Hell No,
Reincarnation?

D1222903

For information about this title or to order other books
and/or electronic media, contact the publisher:
Website: thegiftofpastlives.com

ISBN: 978-1-7343378-2-2 (print)
978-1-7343378-3-9 (eBook)

Printed in the United States of America

Book configuration by 1106 Design

David Bettenhausen and Carla Bogni-Kidd

Hell No, Reincarnation?

with Mother, Isabella, God & Elizabeth

DAVID BETTENHAUSEN
& CARLA BOGNI-KIDD

Dedicated to:

Estes

Gabriel

Isabella

Elizabeth

God

&

Mother

Because their spirit moved us.

Preface

Our first book, *The Gift of Past Lives with Mother, Isabella, God & Elizabeth*, took five years to write as we shared our spiritual experiences and twenty-one of our personal past-life experiences together.

Once our first book was published and received by our family, friends and the public, we realized the need for reconciling our past experiences, religious and spiritual with our new experiences and research. Thus, *Hell No, Reincarnation?* was created.

Seven additional of our past-lives are visited in *Hell No, Reincarnation?* as examples of conflict and karma.

We understand that the subject of reincarnation is controversial and not accepted in all schools of thought. Therefore, we felt it imperative to share our research and others' research in regard to past lives.

This is not the first or second publication about reincarnation, past lives or solid evidence on the subject.

Our need to explore reincarnation is not to oppose the belief of God in fact, it is just the opposite. We believe reincarnation was God's plan from the beginning.

Therefore, we would like to invite you to continue on our quest of spirituality.

Acknowledgments

We would love to thank our friends and family, past and present, who have helped us on our many journeys, our soul family so to speak.

We would love to mention by name those special people who continually share their love and time with us, without judgment or skepticism.

Tom, Paula, Rebecca, Heather, Cheryl Annie, Daisy Elaine, Janet and Brad, Gwen, Diane, Dee, Tim, Ruth Ann, Nicoletta, Marjorie, Rani, Linda, Kevin and the best photo artist on the planet, Ron Pahl Photography.

When writing about such controversial subjects such as reincarnation and past lives, friends can be lost; however, new friends can be found. We have experienced both.

We would love to thank God, yes, God, for each and every experience we have lived. Through those experiences, we have learned about true love and what it is not.

Love,
Dave and Carla

Table of Contents

Part I

A

Alpha

This is not the beginning,
this is the Alpha

Chapter 1
Present vs. Absent God

Whether you are a churchgoer or not and whether you have read the Bible or not, at some point we all ask ourselves: What is the purpose of our life?

If we are asking the purpose of life, we may have wondered about God as well and if God plays a large part in our life.

Who and what is God? What have we learned about God? Most of us know God is perfect, all knowing, merciful, just, loving and a creator. We know this from the Bible, churches, the Quran, the Vedas, other religious books and reading sources.

Is God ever present and the controller of our destiny or is God simply an observer? If God is a mere observer, then, who and what God is, does not matter.

Does God make mistakes? Well, if God is perfect, all knowing and merciful, how can God make mistakes?

This means God must have created us with the potential of reaching perfection. The capability of making choices must be a means of bringing us closer to perfection.

Therefore, if God made us with freedom of choice, it was the way God intended us to be. And with that freedom of choice comes the responsibility for those choices. It belongs to us and us alone. This does not preclude us from making poor choices. God is not forcing us to make those choices, we are. Thus, in God's wisdom, God also created us with the ability to learn. We then learn lessons from poor choices.

When God created us, was there a plan? If there was no plan, then why create us?

Why were we created? God, indeed, had a plan. If God created us with intention, with free will and the ability to learn, then part of the plan must be to exercise our free will and thus learn. How long does that take?

A second? Could our fate truly be determined in one second?

An hour? Would one hour be sufficient to rule our destination?

A day? What could we achieve in only one day?

A year? A year couldn't possibly allow ample time to live all circumstances.

A lifetime? We can certainly know one side of the story.

Many lives? Only in many lifetimes could we learn all other situations.

Eternity? Yes.

So, if we are not eternal or God is dead or just an observer or he doesn't care, then nothing really matters. There is no purpose to our lives. This is nothing but an accident. What becomes of you is meaningless.

If you believe that it is meaningless, then, why are you here in this time?

Our time is not as God's time would appear. What seems a lifetime to us may be a second to God. So, does the infant who dies at birth have any chance to make choices or learn? Is that fair? The infant had no chance to learn or make good choices before returning home to God. Where does that infant go when returning to God?

In some religious circles, to not choose God is to spend eternity in Hell. Did the infant go to Hell?

Dante, the famous writer of Dante's Inferno AD 1300, was a man exiled from his homeland. Alone and on his own spiritual path, he was trying to make sense of that which he did not understand about life and death. Dante decided there must be a place called *Limbo*, where babies go upon death. He couldn't fathom a just God sending them to Hell. Extending Dante's thought from the innocent infant to the learning soul in regard to making choices and growing, we can draw the conclusion God gave us another option than Limbo or Hell.

Each and every soul is unique. If the soul is not unique what purpose would God have for creating it? If every soul is unique then the path that every soul must travel would be unique. Thus, every soul's choices are unique and their own. Every soul's circumstances are also unique and their own. Yet, the kind of circumstances the human must experience are both limited but varied. It is impossible to experience all circumstances and thus all choices in just one lifetime. If we were given more than one choice, why not be given more than one chance? We all grow at different rates. Maybe it takes some of us more than one life. Maybe we are given infinite chances along with infinite choices.

The unique soul can only fully be judged after living a series of circumstances with each judgement being fair, yet unique to that individual specifically.

So, at the end of our life, during reconciliation with God, it's not as simple as you failed or passed. It's not as simple as Heaven or Hell.

It becomes obvious to us that God must not be merely an observer. Because, God plans a unique path for each of us to follow.

Without a great architect involved in our progress the system is incomplete. Each individual is unique, each circumstance is unique, every choice is specific and every potential outcome is considered. Each and every piece, matches, in perfect harmony.

Without the architect, how would each piece fit into the unique design we call destiny? Either creation is an accident, or its destiny.

Is God fair or does God have favorites? If God has favorites, is it fair to be judged by the same criteria as another? Why would God have favorites?

Since each of us is created uniquely, God has a specific, individualized relationship with each of us. Thus, God would judge every individual personally, as God created them. Wouldn't everyone be created with the potential to fulfill their own destiny? If this is true, wouldn't God's plan allow each individual the opportunity to fulfill their destiny? Regardless of how many opportunities a person would need to complete his destiny, God would grant the soul those opportunities.

This is God's plan. This is God's wisdom. This is God's mercy. This is God's justice, and this is God's *love.*

Freedom is one of the cornerstones of happiness. Self-determination or free choice allows us to have control over ourselves. Therefore, to be controlled by another, including God, does not allow you to reach your personal, highest level. If God made all of our choices, how would we learn?

If God told us what to do, how could we choose to *love? Love* that is not given freely is not *love.* And, isn't *love* the basis for all of our actions, either *love* of ourselves or *love* of another. This allows each individual the freedom and choice to *love* God.

God created us. That act of creation was out of God's *love* for each of us. Then, God created us, never to be alone.

Thus, God created us in this world, cohabitating with others we could *love.* God also created angels and spirit guides (or guardian angels) so we would never be alone and to assist us in our individual choices. Angels and spirit guides were created by

God with uniqueness to each individual soul as a direct extension of God's distinctive *love* for each of us.

The Bible mentions angels and many religions have taught us about these extensions of God. Angels and spirit guides are just that, extensions of God here to help us on our individual path. The Hindus believe in Brahma and the many extensions of Brahma which are individual personal counterparts.

Would God create angels, spirit guides or personal counterparts, direct extensions of God if God expected us to fail? Would God reach out to us with assistance, like a tutor in school, with the expectation we would fail and go to Hell?

The direct extension from God in the form of spirit guides and angels is as if God's hand is reaching out for us and holding us. Since God is infallible, why would God ever let go? God never gives up on us. God will never let go.

Since God made it possible for angels and spirit guides to extend their hands to us, figuratively, do we truly believe that God would allow fallen angels the opportunity to extend their hands to us or control us in any manner? God created all; God plans all.

Chapter 2

The Beginning of God's Plan

The Book of Genesis in the Bible talks of the creation of man and the story of the beginning.

It is not our intent to promote creationism or deny evolution. However, the Bible leaves no clues as to who Adam's and Eve's children procreated with to populate the earth. Nor, does it explain the world-wide expansion of human beings. One can only assume Adam and Eve were just one couple of many distributed around the world as originals.

Adam and Eve is just the story of one couple relayed through the years by mouth. In other parts of the world, there existed stories of other couples starting from scratch, learning the ways of living on their own. This explains why different portions of the world developed at different paces, some advanced, some primitive, developing independent of one another.

Some were nomadic (herdsmen, hunters, wanderers) and some were agricultural; even though it appears as though the middle east was an epicenter of growth. The growth actually occurred in areas with temperate climates and water, understandably so.

There is a study of DNA sequencing, concluding that common ancestry of the species Homo sapiens, probably occurring some two hundred thousand years ago, meaning a group of prehumans, could exchange genes and interbreed. The study did not prove that only one original couple produced all other humans. Nor, does it discuss the 194,000 years from the early species to the story of *Adam and Eve*.

DNA sequencing also does not explain the uniqueness and the connection with God that is described in the religious version of the biblical original couple.

Science does support some evidence of evolution. And, the Bible reports the special relationship between God and mankind that occurs at about the time of *Adam and Eve*. Something unique must have happened. It doesn't necessarily mean it only happened once.

■ ■ ■ ■ ■ ■ ■ ■

Some of you may have already read our first book, *The Gift of Past Lives with Mother, Isabella, God & Elizabeth*.

Many years ago, while meditating, we (the authors) had a spontaneous memory of a life in 1925. We were born in the late 1950s. We wondered how it was possible that we both had the same memory of a young flapper and a junior bank executive in Chicago who met at a wedding. The story involved a speakeasy, the mob, murder, deception, family and love. This began our journey into all of our past lives through twenty-nine of them.

So, two coworkers (physician and office manager) went on a journey to learn more about meditation and past life regression. Our discoveries included lives together, as far back as six thousand years ago. Our discoveries sent us further, on a quest for information about reincarnation, karma, religion and our experiences with God.

* * * * * * * *

Meanwhile, miles away in another land...

From the time they were born as Ariela and David on the Mount of Olives, outside of what would become Jerusalem, they realized they were different from their parents and family. This was around six thousand years ago.

Ariela in Hebrew means *Lion of God* and *love* and the Hebrew name Carla, translates to Ariel.

Ariela is one of the authors, Carla. Interestingly that our other author is named David. In Hebrew, David means *beloved*.

Both of our families were part of a seminomadic band. It is said that the trees on the Mount of Olives are some of the oldest and most famous trees in the world, believed to be at least nine hundred years old. David and Ariela were born among those trees.

The evidence of their people was recently excavated in Jerusalem by the Israel Antiquities Authority dating our relatives back seven thousand years. We can only assume this group used a primitive paleo form of the Hebrew language, since written Hebrew did not occur until 1000 BC.

These families cooperated for survival. We would refer to it as instinctual. They were different than the others David and Ariela were, because of their understanding of cooperation versus instinct.

This cooperation was based in Hebrew on *ahav*, meaning *to give* and *Ahava* meaning true love. It is more concerned with giving than receiving. In Hebrew *ahava* is not an emotion but an action.

The young couple soon learned ahava in each other's arms. Others looked at the couple as different. There was something in the couple, not recognizable in themselves. Today, we may say, the couple had a spirited embodiment about them. And, literally, Ariela and David had a spirit/soul in them.

God had intentionally placed them together.

God said, "I will call you Ariela and you shall be his strength and inspiration."

God then said, "I will call you David, and you shall be her love/ahava".

God told Ariela, "Your roots will be as strong as the olive tree and you will bear fruit that will last many generations."

Then, God said, "You will do more together than either of you could accomplish on your own."

David did not see Ariela as **his**. He saw her as the part absent in himself. And, Ariela did not see David as **hers**. She realized that David was the part of herself missing without him.

This is what God wanted and was always meant to be; two working together, becoming one.

David and Ariela set off on a quest. One, to set roots of their own and two, to discover others who had the spirit within them.

They traveled initially west to the area of the Dead Sea. Then, south, along the Dead Sea to the land which would become Moab. They were welcomed by a spirited couple and their children to stay while passing through. While there, Ariela shared with the female part of the couple her lack of bleeding and the feeling of not being herself. Her new friend asked to see her stomach and admitted to having an enlarged stomach also while carrying her child. It would be four months before Ariela and David delivered their first child in their new home.

After leaving their generous, gracious friends, David and Ariela moved along the southern most portion of the Dead Sea close to what would become Neve Zohar. Many streams and springs presented themselves in that area, flowing from the mountains and void of salt. The region was close to the Ein Gedi (a natural reserve), the caves of Qumran, the desert and what would become

David Stream, an area of streams and waterfalls. It is actually viewed as one of the most popular nature sites in the country, presently.

They found refuge and placed their roots. The area was complete with fresh water, green vegetation, steady climate and cave-like accommodations.

David and Ariela welcomed their first child three months after establishing their home. The time approached as Ariela was to begin her confinement or begin the birthing ritual. David found a wild rose in an outcropping of stone next to their shelter. David picked the rose and brought it in to share with Ariela. David had received a message through the Spirit as the rose began to wither and dry up.

The message was as follows: The seed of the rose was strongly planted in the soil. You should nourish the seed and the rose. Just as the Spirit of God has planted a seed in both of you. It is to be nourished with *ahav* (meaning with giving). You cannot own the rose or control it. You must nourish it and provide *ahava*, (love) just as I have nourished you and provided you with the spirit and seed. And, just as I do not own your humanity, for I have given you choice, I still provide and nourish your seed. The combining of man and woman provide the human seed. It is your God who provides the Spiritual seed. For it is you who control the human seed and the human lessons as I control the Spiritual seeds and lessons.

The Spirit seed must grow. It is however, your choice, for the responsibility of your actions lie with you. Those actions, based on *ahava*, allow the seed to mature and grow. Those actions, not based on *ahava*, will cause the seed and flower to wither. The dry seed will then be replanted for I will forgive the actions but you shall still remain responsible. This is your responsibility to nourish your seed with *ahava*. Just as *I AM*, your *I AM*, I will nourish your Spirit seed with *ahava* and forgiveness.

David and Ariela delivered the beautiful, dark-haired daughter with guidance from the Spirit and from experience with birthing baby lambs.

The third farmer harvested all that he had but placed his excess in storage for his future.

God would find favor with both the first and third farmers. Unless the intention of the third farmer was to hoard. God would not find favor in the second farmer who wasted what was given to him and would not have found favor in the selfishness of hoarding.

As the disease of jealousy settled down in the community, the disease of selfishness followed as well as the disease of conceit. For the farmer who put in little effort felt he was entitled to the same reward as the farmers who put in great effort.

Miriam continued to have jealousy for the garden of David and Ariela, ignoring the parable. Covid became angry with the implication that he got what he deserved. Soon, the small community was split.

The choice to *ahava* their neighbor became the choice to hate.

There came a night, because under darkness they believed the Spirit or God could not see them conspire, when Miriam and Covid convinced some of the neighbors that the situation represented an injustice. The moment Miriam, Covid and the other neighbors judged the bounty of another, it darkened their seed. They soon raided David and Ariela's garden. They stole what would have been given freely. And actually, damaged more than would have been needed for their own.

The next day, David and Ariela found the damages to their bountiful garden. The Spirit shared with David who then shared at story-time the following words:

When conceit, jealousy and selfishness become a way of life, it is much like the rose that is picked, withers and dies. The seed must be replanted. For the rose will only flourish when nourished with forgiveness and **ahava***.*

David then stated, "If you take only what you need, without damaging, I will forgive you." Because, this is the lesson that I received.

The others expected retaliation from David and Ariela, not reconciliation. They wrongfully believed that retaliation would provide them with justification to do as they pleased.

Half of the neighbors banded with Covid and Miriam against David and Ariela. They prepared for an entire week to attack David and Ariela. Stakes and spears were made as would have been used for hunting or sacrificing for food of goats and lambs. David and Ariela, all the while, unaware of the preparation.

On the morning of the harvest, the banded neighbors set fire to the garden of David and Ariela and the gardens of the other neighbors who had not joined them. Those who would not join them, would now be dependent on Covid and Miriam. Their garden would now be looked upon as the most beautiful and bountiful of all gardens.

The ownership of the most beautiful and bountiful garden would exalt them above all the others.

When David and Ariela tried to fight the fire, Covid and Miriam thought their plan might fail. So, they hurled spears at their family, killing four of their children.

Miriam ordered Covid to send a spear at David. Ariela jumped in front of the spear meant for David to save his life in her last act of *ahava*. Ariela was forty-eight years old.

David reached Ariela as she lay dying in his arms that day. She spoke only two words: *Ahav* and *ahava*.

Idella, Mesa, Martha and Ilmi, two sons and two daughters of David and Ariela were murdered that day. Idella was twenty-six years of age, Mesa twenty-four, Martha twenty-two and Ilmi fourteen. Idella's two children were killed alongside her as she attempted to extinguish the fire. Although Johanna lived, her husband Matthew was killed also that day. Their son became known as Matthew in remembrance of his father.

David was left to raise and care for the remainder of their children. Cintha was just eight years old, Hallena was thirteen,

Kahlia was seventeen and Johanna eighteen years of age. The older children still remaining were Arcella twenty-one, Orchid twenty-five, Aris twenty-seven and Rose twenty-nine years of age, all present with their families that day.

The husband of Martha, Jerome, was aware of the plot that day as he was one that had banded against David and Ariela. Although he had chosen not to participate in the burning of the gardens he also chose not to tell his wife what was planned. He lost his wife during the fight and then later threw himself off the waterfall at David's Stream in despair, leaving his two children without parents.

The next morning, unbeknown to David, their daughter Kahlia, visited the shelter of Covid and Miriam. While Covid slept off the effects of the previous night's celebration, she pretended to have concern for Miriam. Kahlia told Miriam that her father did not plan retribution since too many had already died. Kahlia offered Miriam food as an act of kindness, and as Kahlia cut up the food, she turned on Miriam, grabbing her, and cutting off her hair. She spoke, "Now your ugliness mirrors the ugliness you left behind." Kahlia turned to leave as Miriam grabbed her. Kahlia thrust the knife into her chest, killing her. She noticed Miriam's and Covid's infant son nearby. Kahlia had no children at that time and the infant now had no mother. She could not imagine leaving him with the man who had caused such damage. She stole the child, returned to her family camp and raised him as her own. His name was Hileal.

David traveled by caravan, taking his entire family and their spouses, children and grandchildren to what would become Syria, west of the Sea of Galilee. He lived out the remainder of his days until the actual age of 102, without Ariela. Even though he was sorrowful and angry, he remained committed to *ahav* and *ahava*.

Three days after the death of Ariela, David could feel her presence which remained with him throughout his life.

Ariela's seed was again planted. Because of an early death, she had not been allowed to completely nourish her Spirit.

And, so began the battle between jealousy, conceit, selfishness and unforgiveness, versus love. In war, there is always a winner and a loser. However, the winner always loses also.

Lessons learned during this lifetime...

- The murderer always gathers negative karma.
- The one who is killed has their ability to learn and to grow taken away.
- It is the choice or action of each individual that matters.
- Apparently, God allows bad choices. There are no mistakes. Just negative choices.
- A negative choice or negative karma forces learning and growth to follow.
- God planted the seed, yet we reap what we sow.
- Jealousy, conceit and selfishness are always related to negative choices.
- Revenge or retaliation cannot be justified by you, under any circumstances.
- Judgement and restitution belong to God.
- This leads us to one question…is forty-eight years enough, is twenty-six enough, is twenty-four enough, is twenty-two enough, is fourteen enough, are months on Earth enough time to completely learn and grow? Apparently, those seeds were replanted too.

If we are worrying about the state of the world in the future, why are we not worrying about the state of our soul in the future? Every choice we make involves everyone and everything around us.

All things go through stages or cycles.

A seed grows to a seedling. A seedling grows to a tree. A tree drops a seed. The tree dies and fertilizes for the next seed. Thus, as the tree plants its seeds, the soul plants the seed or karma for its next existence. Even if we die, the seed has already been planted.

Our soul is not our seed. But we reap what we sow. Our seed is our karma.

Just like the tree, woman/man passes from seed to embryo to child, to adult, to death and back again to seed.

Do we judge the tree that provides shade differently from the tree that does not? Do we judge the tree that provides fruit, different from the tree that does not? Yet, the tree fulfilled its purpose and created a seed. Does either tree die and go to Hell?

Does life stop without the seed? Yes, just as life stops without the soul.

Does a tree die without growth, fruit or nuts? Yes.

Can the horticulturist modify a tree to create a new type of tree? Yes. Just as the soul can be modified by the seeds planted by us, thus our karma follows us and our seed.

Who planted our seed? We did. Not God, not fallen angels, not cosmic chance.

Do we care what seed we are planting? Do we think God cares? Why else would God give us chance after chance to plant the seeds correctly?

You may have heard of the farmer and his seeds from a popular publication. It's called the "Parable of the soils."

The farmer throws his seeds on barren ground. Some fall on the path, where no soil is seen. Some fall on rocky ground with little soil. Some fall on ground with many thorns and weeds. These three cases fail to produce a crop. When the seed falls on good soil, it grows, yielding sixty-fold.

The moral of the parable is the soul, like the good soil, is created by God. No matter what the seed is, it will grow in the soil or the soul.

Chapter 4
The Soul

The *soul* is your essence, created before you were born. Therefore, you still have an essence after you die or are done. Without a soul, you have no vessel to carry your karma.

Wind can be felt but not seen until it moves something. God is breathing your soul into your body. It can be felt more than seen, until it moves you.

Realizing, of course, it can be felt but it doesn't mean anything until there is an action. For example, **love** is both a feeling and an action. Without a response, it means nothing.

According to James Blackburn, a Catholic Apologist, Author and Speaker, who holds a master's degree in Theology from John Paul the Great Catholic University, the soul is the spiritual principle of human beings. The soul is the subject of human consciousness and freedom; soul and body together form one unique human nature. Each human soul is individual and immediately created by God. The soul does not die with the body, from which it is separated by death and with which it will be reunited in the final resurrection.

If this is the case, how was it possible in the Bible, Matthew 17, when Jesus took Peter, James and John up on a high mountain by themselves that Moses and Elijah appeared to them, while talking to Jesus. How did they know it was Moses and Elijah? Was it because they were recognizable still in their Earth suit? Who recognized them? Peter, James, John and Jesus were not alive while Moses and Elijah were.

Supposedly Elijah was taken to Heaven without ever dying according to 2 Kings 2. So, he remains in his body as it was, forever? He was taken up in a whirlwind or a chariot of fire.

The Bible does say that Moses died. You may argue that Elijah died and kept his body but how can you say that Moses died and kept his body also? Is there or is there not a day when we will all be resurrected with our bodies?

We are separated from our bodies at death if we follow the beliefs of the Catholic Church and the Bible. According to the Catholic teachings, Mary of Nazareth, at the end of her earthly life, was raised with her body directly into Heaven. Why are there so many exceptions? Which parts of the Bible are we to follow and believe to the letter?

Elijah, who Jesus states is John the Baptist in Matthew 11:14, could have been recognized by Jesus, if he resembled John the Baptist, Jesus's cousin.

Was John the Baptist already dead when Jesus recognized Elijah on the mountain? We will have to assume that John was already dead. But, why wouldn't Jesus recognize him as his cousin John instead of Elijah?

Either way, why did Elijah and Moses have bodies? Or does our body die, and our soul go to God, awaiting Atonement? What purpose does our body serve? What value does our body have? Isn't it our soul God values? God created our soul. The body is temporary. The soul is eternal.

So, considering all of the people who have already died, since the beginning, let us get this perfectly clear. Enoch, who's Gnostic book was removed from the Bible and Elijah and Mary of Nazareth had died and went directly to Heaven with their bodies. Jesus, who died, was placed back in his body and ascended to Heaven. Thus, of all the people who have died, only four souls have their bodies in Heaven. Why?

And, why does Moses appear to Jesus, Peter, James and John when the doctrine clearly states, people who died before Jesus have yet to be judged and are waiting for Jesus's death to be saved? Did God make an exception? There appears to be many exceptions.

Apparently, there has been some confusion on exactly what happens to the soul and the body when we die.

So, the soul, religions believe to be eternal? All major faiths believe the soul leaves the body and moves onto another existence. Some believe that means they go to paradise or Hell. And, others believe that a soul may achieve another rebirth, meaning into another physical body. A body is merely what a person has, but not what a person is.

Modern biblical theologians believe the Old Testament made no references to the soul being immortal. They also reject the Bible view teaching the doctrine of an immortal soul. Many Christians are unhappy with the new beliefs.

It was actually the Christian scholar Origen of Alexandria around AD 200 who taught that our immortal soul was created before birth and remained after death. Origen also taught transmigration of the soul or, in other words, reincarnation. He was considered to be one of the Church Fathers. But he was tortured for his refusal to sacrifice to Roman Gods by Emperor Decius AD 250. In AD 453, because of his belief in reincarnation, the Emperor Justinian 1 condemned him as a heretic and ordered all his writings be burned.

Let's see...the man they based almost all of the Christian doctrine on, Origen of Alexandria, died a Christian martyr, and was excommunicated from the church two hundred years later for his following beliefs and teachings which were: the human soul exists before conception, the human soul enters a different body after death and the reign of God will be restored once the world ends. Is the Christian church then stating that God won't rule the world at the end? We are so confused.

How about if we simplify this?

Why do we need a soul? We only need a soul if we are eternal and or we live more than one life. Otherwise, we have no reason to exist after death. The real question here is, why are the soul and the body considered two separate parts? Why can't they be one, together, if they have only one existence? There's no purpose for their separation unless the soul does, indeed, have another purpose. If the soul can separate from the body, the soul can carry your responsibility forward into another life. Thus, the soul is a record and vessel for karma.

The soul in psychology is partially subconscious and partially conscious. Our conscious self experiences us through our five senses. The soul experiences through the five senses and then, most literally, the sixth sense, *love*. *Love* really is the definition of karma. Those things that bring us closer to *love*, are what we would call good karma. Those things that bring us farther from *love*, we call bad karma. Then again, what the soul experiences at times, are part of our five senses. That is our worldly experience. But the soul really experiences all things based on *love*. This was God's gift; the gift of *love*.

So, it's the soul that is the reservoir and it is what is our essence. Thus, our karma really is our essence of *love*.

When we experience anything that is based on another, it is how our karma will be affected and how it affects our choices. If we make a decision based on *love*, it affects the positive karma that is recorded in our soul. If we make a decision based on selfishness, jealousy, conceit, or unforgiveness and all the forms of those things, it impresses upon our soul. This is the record of the essence of what is us, recorded through karma based on *love.*

God's creation is a creation of *love.* It is based on a fulfillment of potential, growth, change and choice; a choice that involves the soul, taking the soul to a higher place.

This is all part of the evolution of the soul.

Chapter 5
Potential

*I*f we believe in God, and that God is involved in our lives, we must believe we are here for a purpose, an outcome or a potential.

So, let's clarify what this means. Either we are brought to Earth for a reason, to accomplish something or to assist someone in an accomplishment or we are brought to Earth to interact with another. However, it cannot only be the accomplishment or the interaction which matters. It very much has to be the intention behind the action that matters. Intentions are the why we are accomplishing.

Most religious thoughts are based on a theory of moral code. That could be the Ten Commandments, The Word of Wisdom, the Quran, etc.

Thou Shalt Not Kill. It doesn't mean we cannot defend ourselves but it does mean we cannot kill another human, without reason. Certainly, intent matters. Therefore, the "why" we do things does matter. If what we do and why we do it matters, it must affect our outcome, or our potential outcome.

As far as God is concerned, it's impossible not to be caught! What God catches us at must affect us at either judgement or at what we call karma or both.

This brings up an interesting point. In basic religious thought, there's a point where we come to maturity. Whether that means enlightenment or we are saved, the religious theory says once enlightened or saved, all our past actions, or intentions no longer matter. What about our actions after we are saved, enlightened or whatever you call it?

If we are baptized at seven days, eight months or nine years old, we technically are far from maturity in all ways. Even if we undergo another sacrament at about age twelve, twenty-five, twenty-eight or at death what happens after we have arrived at that holy state? What if we make a bad choice after that sacrament? What if we are saved at fifty? And then at sixty, we go through a twelve-step program and five years later we fall off the proverbial wagon. Are we doomed to Hell?

What if we intended to have pure intentions? We tried. We got help. We are only human. Does God take any of that into consideration? Or, nope, God just says, "Go to Hell."

Or, we could just be saved again! Then, the question arises, "How often can we be saved?"

So, which actions affect our potential outcome? Apparently, only God can decide. We can only probably argue that God decides based on our potential. When God created us, wasn't God already aware of our potential?

If God knew our potential or outcome, would we have been created to just end up in Hell?

We have all heard of being saved by the grace of God. We are all sinners. Yet, God must believe that even sinners have potential. Because, even as humans, we must believe after we die there is still potential, for how often do we pray for those who have died before us?

We have even created the idea of Limbo and Purgatory. This means we can continue to grow, be enlightened or saved even after we die.

The definition of Purgatory is a place or state of suffering inhabited by the souls of sinners who are expiating their sins before going to heaven. Wait, we thought if we sinned, we went to Hell?

And, the definition of Limbo is the supposed abode of souls of unbaptized infants, and of the *Just*, who died before Christ's coming.

What a minute. So, all those *dead infants* and all the *Just* have to wait in Limbo until Jesus returns? Definition of *Just: "Based on or behaving according to what is morally right and fair."*

So, when Jesus went up the mountain with Peter and James in Matthew 17:2, and was transfigured and standing with Elijah and Moses, they must be appearing from Limbo? Apparently, the dead can communicate with the living? It's just a simple question.

How were Elijah and Moses back in their bodies? Isn't the second coming of Jesus when souls are reconnected with their bodies?

After some thousand years of decay, we can only imagine, this, as, something from *The Walking Dead.*

Definition of absurd: "Wildly unreasonable, illogical, or inappropriate. Arousing amusement or derision; ridiculous."

According to the Hebrew Bible, She'ol is a place of darkness to which all the dead go, both the righteous and the unrighteous, regardless of the moral choices made in life, a place of stillness and darkness cut off from and separated from God. She'ol means "the grave."

We must believe then, that She'ol or Purgatory or Limbo is a place somewhere between the beginning and the end.

Doesn't that insinuate that every soul doesn't go straight to Heaven or Hell at death? Another religious theory is that there is a preexistence of the soul before birth along with the theory that we are immortal souls. There, perhaps, appears to be a place in between Heaven and Hell and the beginning and the end.

We know we are tested at least once while on Earth. Why not more than once? Could Earth be known as Purgatory? Again, the definition of Purgatory is a place or state of suffering inhabited by the souls of sinners (which is all of us) who are expiating their sins before going to Heaven. Definition of expiating means, "To Atone."

What does Atonement mean? It means reparation for a wrong or injury. Now, we return to the meaning of "Potential." Potential is defined as having or showing the capacity to become or develop into something in the future; latent qualities or abilities that may be developed and lead to future success or usefulness. Again, we'll just bring back the reference to nature, evolution and cycling.

And then, what is the definition of Karma? It is defined as the sum of a person's actions in this and the previous state of existence, viewed as deciding their fate in future existence, destiny or fate, following as effect from cause.

This sounds like the work of Atonement, Purgatory, or Reincarnation. So, God created us knowing we had potential and why would God create us if it wasn't possible for us to reach our potential?

If you have read with comprehension the definitions above, it is apparent that the Soul can evolve and possibly takes more than the time of one lifetime to reach its full potential.

■ ■ ■ ■ ■ ■ ■ ■

Blossoming potential...

Sometimes potential starts as small children. Sometimes, it's in a little girl who grew to be one of the richest queens of England. Sometimes, it also begins with a little boy who followed his father to work early every day, to watch that little girl who walked the entire garden each morning.

At the end of the garden, there grew a circular patch of red roses with one single, white rose bush growing directly in the center. The little girl habitually meandered through the entire garden and then circled the patches of roses.

Each day she watched the workers of the estate arrive upon reaching the rose patch. Once she saw the workers coming, she turned and ran the entire length of the cobblestoned path back to the manor. This was her daily routine.

Each day, the little boy watched her run and wished he could run to catch her. But each time, his father restrained his wish.

His father was always the first worker to arrive on the estate. It seemed like every day it was a bit earlier. And every day, his father was perturbed, with garden shears in hand, that the little girl had already begun her ritual.

It seems that Richard had requested that Hugon's father plant the patch of roses for his wife and once their daughter Emma was born, he again requested a single white rose bush be planted in the center.

Hugon's father's concern was that there never be a wilted rose in the patch, red or white. Yet, young Emma continued to beat him to the patch, elevating his concern that she would detect a dying rose before he could.

Four rows of lowly trimmed hedges led to the manor. A cobble-stone path lay between the middle two.

Hugon

As I approached my tenth birthday, I experienced two memorably beautiful experiences in the garden. One evening as the sun set, my father took me just outside the front door of the manor. It happened to be the end of the cobblestone path. He advised me to kneel on the path and to look to the west, down the path. The sun seemed to set directly on the rose bushes.

When kneeling, it appeared as if the red of sunset and the red of the roses were one. My father told me, "Whatever you do, always remember to look, for there is only one day per year for the potential of the sunset to align perfectly with the rose bushes and blend together."

So, I asked my father why I had to kneel and he responded, "Hugon, sometimes we must humble ourselves before God and nature to truly enjoy the beauty." My father then knelt beside me, pulled out his shears and trimmed the very bottom edge of a one of the hedges. He realized I was questioning him with an interested stare. He said, "Like father, like son. Someday, this garden will be yours to tend. I have learned to look at the bushes from many perspectives. If I had not once knelt to trim the bottom of the bush, I would not have seen the beauty of the sunset as it melted into the red of the hedges."

The next morning, my father awakened me before sunrise. He handed me the rose clippers and advised me to run to the garden before the little girl arrived. I ran as fast as I could possibly run. The sun was barely peeking over the horizon. There was one pedal on the white rose bush turning to brown. I pulled the pedal from the stem and saw the door to the front of the manor begin to open. I crouched as low as I possibly could as the little girl came sauntering through the garden.

She had curls at the ends of her long, blond hair. The white collar of her dress was stiffly pressed. From my vantage point, now kneeling, the white on the collar of her dress and the white from the single white rose bush, blended together as one. Her face was full like the sun, that I had seen the night before. I could no longer restrain myself. I popped up from my knees, not knowing the proper etiquette or way to address the girl of the manor. I simply touted, "Hi Emma."

Emma stood in shock, from surprise but also from my bold greeting. A young man was never to be alone with a young woman. A common gardener's son should never be allowed with the girl of the manor. Emma bent over and picked up the brown pedal which had been plucked from the white rose bush and allowed to fall to the ground. Emma said, "I've walked here every morning for the past year looking for imperfection. What if I report this to my father?"

I tried to think of a quick response. I said, "It must be a matter of perspective. From where I stand, the rose bush looks perfect."

Then, she smiled and walked toward me. She placed the rose pedal in my hand. She asked my name and I responded, "Hugon."

"I will remember that, Hugon. Thank you," she said.

It felt as if her fingers lingered in the palm of my hand as she placed the brown rose pedal in my clutches. My face flushed to a bright red, the color of the rose bushes and sunset. She turned and walked with a grace not familiar to me. This time, she did not run down the path as so often I had witnessed.

She did not turn around once she'd begun her walk down the cobblestone path. However, I clearly heard her say, "Hugon, I appreciate your perspective on beauty and your smile."

I stood and watched as she walked away. This time there was a change in the little, young girl, who I used to watch run away.

The following morning, I was up and dressed before dawn. Again, I ran to the rose garden of my father's employer. I now understood my father's frustration. For, there she was, already standing next to the rose bushes.

Differently than the past year, as the employees began to arrive, myself included, Emma did not turn and run but rather lingered in the garden.

I approached the rose bushes and began the examination of their pedals. "Hugon," pointing she said, "I believe the petal right there is starting to curl." I removed the petal she believed to be curling.

She looked straight at me, saying, "How come the toes on both of your shoes are so scuffed?" My response was, "Sometimes, I have to kneel and these are the only shoes I own."

Then, I saw another rose pedal with imperfection. I knelt next to the rose bush and said while gazing up into her face, "Sometimes you have to kneel to get the true perspective of the beauty." Her face flushed nearly as much as mine had the day before.

Much to my surprise, Emma knelt in the mud next to me. I was astonished by her actions. I had spoken with my father and knew I was not of her station. I said, "My lady, you should not be kneeling in a garden." She responded with, "Just once, I would like to see this garden from your perspective."

Emma reached over and took my hand as we remained kneeling in the garden. I whispered under my breath, "Emma, what are you doing?" Emma answered, "Hugon, I am praying that someday I will feel something this beautiful again."

Her head came ever closer to mine, as she kissed me on my lips. She stood up and attempted to look as the graceful woman who had walked the cobblestone path the night before but, instead, she started to run away much like the young girl I had first seen.

The next morning, I again arose before dawn. Once reaching the rose garden, I noticed Emma was nowhere to be found. I thought, "I have finally arrived before her to the garden."

I quickly began examining the rose bushes and their pedals. I could find not one imperfection. Yet, I stayed kneeling in the garden.

Emma did not come. In fact, Emma never came back to the garden again.

My father explained to me about the betrothal of Emma to the King of England. Her father, Richard the Fearless and his wife Gunnor, of Viking/Danish descent, had promised and delivered their daughter to the King of England at her young age of eleven. The union was an attempt to join Saxon, England, with Normandy and the Vikings. Emma was married to King Æthelred the Unready, by the age of twelve, he being thirty years old.

The *potential* first seen in the garden between Hugon and Emma never materialized. Although Emma became a beloved queen, the promised potential of a Saxon, Norman, Viking truce, never occurred. War never ended. Emma's second husband was a warrior Viking king, known as Cnut The Great. Emma, once again, agreed unwillingly to marry the Viking king in an attempt to unite England and to save the lives of her sons.

Hugon continued to care for the garden belonging to Emma's parents, every morning arriving before dawn. And, every morning he knelt in the rose garden, slowly pruning the flowers. Each day, after pruning the roses, he would turn and look down the cobblestone path once again watching for Emma to arrive. If ever Emma would return, Hugon carefully manicured the rose garden to perfection, never wanting her to find it any other way.

What once drew David and Ariela together never reached its potential in Hugon and Emma. Outside sources consisting of greed and power, or conceit if you will, interfered with love. Jealousy over land and war, also intervened.

The English could not forgive the Danish and the Danish could not forgive the English. Out of pure selfishness, they could not share the lands they had inhabited together.

Lessons learned in this lifetime...

- When conceit, selfishness and jealousy interfere, love is lost.

- Emma's parents could not see the beauty of their garden but rather the beauty in power and greed.

- People (woman or girls) are not to be owned or sold, given for money or power.

- Hugon devoted his life to waiting for Emma, never loving again. The possibility of love was lost.

Chapter 6
Conflict, Inside and Out

Conflict by definition is a struggle between people which could be physical or between conflicting ideas. It can also be within one person, or it can involve several people. Conflicts begin because of needs, values or ideas that are believed to be different and there seems to be no way to reconcile the difference.

There are five main forms of conflict:

- Type 1—Informational conflicts. People have insufficient information or widely differing experiences. Another good reason for the cause of karmic debt and reincarnation.

- Type 2—Value conflicts. People have perceived or have actual incompatible belief systems. People or a group attempt to impose their values upon another. Of course, this is another argument for reincarnation. If you have not yet learned or experienced another's belief system, how would you learn? This is the basis for conceit.

- Type 3—Interest conflicts. These are caused through competition. Usually, the cause is due to resources, time or money. This is the basis of jealousy.

- Type 4—Relationship conflicts. This occurs when there are misconceptions, strong negative emotions or poor communications. This is related to distrust, most often.

- Type 5—Structural conflicts. These types of conflicts are caused by oppressive behaviors exerted on others. Frequently, they are organizationally structured and a power structure, based on position. This is based on conceit, or the right of position.

Informational conflicts. You haven't lived it and therefore cannot possibly understand another's situation. This is just misinformation. You cannot understand what you do not know! This is based on "I" not another.

Value conflicts. You may have belief in a subject due to your upbringing or based only on your personal experience, not based on another's. This conflict is the basis for racism, religious persecution, gender bias, nationalism etc. This is based on "us" not them.

Interest conflicts. We want what we want, when we want it and we are angry if someone else has what we want! This is based on "I" not another.

Relationship conflicts. This is based on an assumption of malice or inequity. Relationships are usually based on an assumption of partnership; partners meaning equal to. Based on a *give* and *take* experience. Unfortunately, either or both partners believe they are giving more than 50 percent to the relationship, unsubstantiated. Again, this is based on "I" not us.

Structural conflicts. Organizational conflicts based on hierarchy or based on position presents a unique type of discord. Based on definition, this is based on inequality. This is based on "you" not me.

Interestingly enough, some of the synonyms for conflict are: battle, combat, competition, rivalry, struggle and *war*. This sums it up. *In war, no one wins.*

■　■　■　■　■　■　■　■

Values conflicted in religion...

Around the year of AD 1150 in Antioch, Turkey, there lived a woman named Constance of Hauteville. She ruled as the princess of Antioch. She was the only child of Bohemond II of Antioch and his wife Alice of Jerusalem. Her father had fallen in battle when Constance was just two years of age. The noblemen of Antioch had replaced her as the acting regent because of her gender. Baldwin II of Jerusalem was Constance's grandfather and replacement. Upon the death of Baldwin II, Alice attempted to assume her rightful place as the queen. The barons of Antioch acknowledged her brother-in-law, Fulk of Angou, to rule as the regent for Constance until her reaching maturity.

Alice tried to marry Constance off to the son of a Byzantine emperor, John the II Komnenos's, son Manuel without success. The noblemen had already chosen her husband along with Fulk of Angou. Raymond of Pointiers, the younger son of William IX, Duke of Aquitaine, was disguised and brought to marry Constance. The decision to stop the marriage of the Byzantine son to Constance was due to the power which would have been created between a Roman Catholic and Byzantine-Catholic marriage.

The Catholic church had been split into two separate religions, Eastern Orthodox and Roman Catholic during the Great Schism of 1054. The Byzantine empire then became Eastern Orthodox. The area had been too large to be controlled by one pope. The Roman Catholics wanted to remain in control not forfeiting any power to the Byzantines.

Constance was given, not by choice, in marriage in AD 1136 to Raymond of Poitiers at the age of eight years old. Raymond, based on his gender, ruled Antioch until AD 1149. Raymond was thirty-seven. They had four children in eleven years.

After Raymond was murdered in war, Fulk of Angou's son, Baldwin III of Jerusalem, assumed the regency over Constance once again. He attempted to convince Constance to remarry a middle-aged relative to which she refused.

There had been too much concern from the noblemen on Constance finding the appropriate spouse. There had been frequent dinners introducing Constance to available men. The majority of the potential suiters were many years her senior.

Raynald of Chatillon had been of lesser nobility but had attended a dinner as part of an entourage of possible suiters. Constance saw Raynald as nobility, Catholic and young which was enough to keep her attention. Raymond had been twenty-nine years older than Constance and arranged.

When Constance was twenty-five years old and Raynald was twenty-eight, they had met. Raynald already had leadership skills in war. He could have been considered a French mercenary to the Catholic church. Since war was their way of life, a strong, young man was attractive to Constance for marriage. This time, she chose passion over political correctness as well. They married in 1153. Eventually, Constance did find love in the marriage to Raynald of Chatillon who was from a French noble family. They together raised Constance's children from her first marriage, Bohemond

III, Maria, Raimond and Phillippa as well as their own children Baldwin III of Antioch and Agnes of Antioch.

Raynald fell into captivity in AD 1160 during the wars of the Second Crusade by the governor of Aleepo, the largest city in Syria. Raynald was held in prison. He was accused of trying to make too much money for himself.

After Raynald's incarceration, Constance's son Bohemond III was of majority age and made regent instead of Constance. She was later forced to leave Antioch due to her nonsupport of her son's reign. She was unable to gain support of the other noblemen to rule in her husband's absence. She fled toward Jerusalem. It is rumored that her envoy was intercepted by Muslim invaders. She was decapitated for being a Catholic not Muslim in 1163. It is believed that the rumors reached her husband Raynald who was not released from captivity until 1176. This increased his vigilance against the Muslim crusades.

He never returned to Antioch, due to the murder of his wife.

Raynald led the Crusades that defeated Saladin, the first Sultan of Egypt and Syria. Saladin led the Muslim military crusade against the Catholic crusader states of which Raynald was part of.

At his high point Saladin was the caliphate (or religious Muslim King) of Egypt, Syria, Mesopotamia, Yemen and a large part of north Africa. Although Raynald could have used religious crusades as his reason for going to war after his wife's death, but he had been given control over much of the caravan routes between Egypt and Syria which meant he had control over the major financial flow of supplies, his wealth and his vengeance. He was hiding beneath religion as a reason to control and retaliate.

Raynald was captured in AD 1187 and brought before the Caliphate Saladin once again with one of the other officers. Guy of Lucignan was offered a cup of iced, rose water by Saladin. Guy handed the water to Raynald as an Islam custom. The Muslim custom to hand food or drink to a prisoner meant you could not murder them. So, Saladin turned to Raynald and stated, "It is Guy who has given you the cup." He then accused Raynald of blasphemy and gave him a choice. "You may choose between turning to Islam or die," he said. Raynald flatly refused to convert. Saladin struck him with a sword, dropping him to the ground then beheading him. Raynald's head was brought to Damascus and dragged along the ground for all to witness and to mark that vengeance had been imposed by Saladin.

Lessons learned in this lifetime...

- Conflict of war can be caused by any number of issues whether it's related to your belief system, interests, or structure. Whether it is the Catholics over the Muslims or the location of the trade route, or whether it is the right of birth or position, conflict begins.

- In war there is always a winner and always a loser; however, in war, even the winner loses.

- It creates an inequality between genders when one is chosen over the other simply based on their sex. Men do not rule more powerfully than women. They have no guarantees just for being male.

- There are no rights that come with birthplace. There are no birthrights. We are all unique and none of us more special. A body or a country is merely where the soul is placed. A woman has no rulership rights based on who her parents are or were.

If Constance and Raynald are David and Ariela reseeded, they must have learned the other side of war and jealousy, conceit and self-ishness but at what cost? They did not completely lose everything. They kept **ahava**. *However, considering the karmic debt of murder, conceit, jealousy and selfishness, they would still need to be reseeded. Since their lives were again cut short, complete **ahava** was unable to grow and could not overcome their karma.*

■ ■ ■ ■ ■ ■ ■ ■

Values conflicted in relationships...

Around 3400 BC a child was born in Ethiopia. Her name was Corna. Lucy, the famous, believed to be first, female Homo sapiens was discovered in Ethiopia. She apparently lived about one-hundred-sixty thousand years before Corna.

Scientists were, indeed, able to trace one of the earliest forms of Homo sapiens to Ethiopia (Lucy). Was Corna a descendent of this Homo sapiens? How does this contrast with two other lives we know about, Adam and Eve, who really lived about six-hundred years before Corna was born? The possible proposed location of the Garden of Eden is in an area of southern Iraq where the Tigris and the Euphrates rivers run into the sea. In the year 4000 BC, the world's Homo sapiens population was six million. Something happened in 4000 BC to populate to that extreme density of the new Homo sapiens, other than just one couple, Adam and Eve.

David and Ariela lived at the same time as the Garden of Eden. How was the world's population spread out so fast? How many other couples were created during that same time?

Corna was born into a family of four. Her family moved from Ethiopia to what is now Turkey, following the waterways north to settle. But before they moved from Ethiopia, her mother Mana, was the leader of a cult that worshipped the divine female God, Aso. The cult practiced monotheism. They believed that Mother God was the creator of all things and nature. They believed all women to be extensions of Aso as evidenced by their ability to create new life. Their beliefs also were that nature provided healing. Therefore, they practiced an early version of *herbal medicine.*

Mana's cult was not viewed in positivity by other masculine-driven tribal cults. Because women held the positions of power due to their beliefs in Aso, it created disbelief in Mana. Those cults accused Mana and her followers of casting spells with her herbs in an early form of witchcraft. However, they could still easily believe in their own medicine men using the same herbs.

The men in Mana's tribe found joy in servitude to the women of the tribe because it expressed servitude to their God, Aso. Resistant men of the tribe were often made more docile by the use of herbs. This was a practice learned by all the women.

Docile men do not always make the best warriors. Thus, Mana's tribe was threatened with war from the adjacent tribes and the control they posed.

The other tribesmen wanted to possess the females of Mana's tribe to control that which they could not have. Although Mana's tribesmen were sometimes docile it was due, in part, to her teaching that war and battle served no purpose. Mana's justification was, by their very nature, that men were violent.

Although the tribesmen were nonviolent, they were still creative and exceptional builders of boats.

Mana eventually fled with her tribespeople in lieu of war. They used the boats built by her men to travel north by the Red Sea to the Mediterranean Sea and on to Turkey. They chose not to stop earlier than Turkey, passing through Palestine, a very male-dominant area, believing in a Father God.

Mana's people reached the area of Turkey that believed differently and also in many Gods. However, the belief in a female God was not threatening. The strict teachings of a divine female God was kept secret by her tribe in the beginning. Mana then began teaching the divine-female teachings only to the women. The males could be Godless and with that able to be controlled and kept docile. Mana encouraged her daughters and all the other young tribeswomen to marry outside of the tribe for protection. It was safer to marry a young, trained warrior to keep docile than to marry a docile man without warrior training.

Corna, at the age of twenty-one, had completed her training and had saved her creativity (virginity) as required by her mother. She met a man from another tribe named Saga. He was tall and strong of body but short of mind. Corna by that age was craving of the body and not particularly interested in the mind. She had been taught that the mind could be controlled.

Saga's interests also laid with the body and not in the mind. His mind was easy to wander, however. They soon took up a relationship together and bore a daughter.

Corna had no appreciation of his aggressive behavior although it somewhat attracted her in the beginning. She also did not appreciate his wandering eye. Corna attempted to apply an herbal remedy for his roaming eyes.

Saga became apathetic or unmotivated under the influence of Corna's potion or was it in all actuality the lack of conquest in Corna. He had no interest in Corna but remained interested in other women.

She began to lessen the dose of the herbal remedy. Along with restoring his potency toward her it restored his aggression; especially when Saga learned of Corna's potion. In a fit of rage over his discovery, he strangled Corna to death.

Mana realized then that having untrained men with no fear of God, was a fatal mistake. And, as war broke out, most of her tribesmen were killed. Soon, the only thing remaining was the myth of Aso which blossomed into the myth of the Goddess Isis.

———

Lessons learned during this lifetime...

- This type 4 conflict in a relationship cannot be controlled pharmacologically. A relationship based on deceit, control and inequality is doomed to failure or death.

- Removing God from 50 percent of the population sets up conflict type 2. Their belief system and value systems are very different. One is based on *I* rather than *us*.

- Conceit and control from within will destroy just as quickly as a war on the outside.

- Love does not exist unless given freely.

- Love is a gift that must be given and not taken.

- Religion is not an excuse to restrict free choice. Free choice is given by God.

- No portion of society owns God.

- A life cut short must be reseeded.

A flawed theology, no matter how well-meaning, can only add to your karmic debt. Even though the theology of nonwar and pacification with respect for the divine female has merit it ignores the divine completeness of God. The same could be said for a religion based only on a male God. This, too, would ignore the completeness of God.

■　■　■　■　■　■　■　■

Values conflicted between countries...

As I ride on, I am dry, dusty, thirsty and tired. We have trained and traveled to the northernmost corner of England, to Falkirk, it is 1298. My horse is sturdy and strong. She has been with me for five years.

I am remembering the day I met William. I was wearing a small, leather, floppy hat. I remember my hat because William's hat was pressed velvet. I wasn't much more than a small, poor farm boy and he was a man of means. The only thing that I could have compared to his was a dark chestnut horse that I had groomed to perfection.

I really do not remember why we had that first conversation or why I agreed to race him around the mulberry tree at the end of the meadow. I do know that he was quite pompous and laughed at the thought that I could beat him. But sometimes it is the communication with your horse and the man on top that truly matters.

That day, I rode with a wild abandonment and when I rounded the mulberry tree, I was already a horse length ahead. By the time we returned to the beginning of the meadow, I had outdistanced him by sixty feet. I swung and jumped down from my horse as he finally crossed the finish line. And, when he finally got down from his horse, I was annoyed to see the pompous ass laughing. He said, "I have found very few men that could outride me like that. The king is looking for experienced horsemen." He said, "You and your horse move as one."

That night, I watered and fed my horse. I brushed her down one last time. For tomorrow, I would meet my destiny. I would fight for my king against the barbarian Scotsmen. I polished my sword, I prayed and I laid my head upon the ground. With my eyes closed, all I could see was a blond, fair-eyed beauty I called Penelope. I hoped the other men would not see the tear on my cheek.

In the morning, William found me. We had become strange friends of sort. I but five feet eight and William almost six feet five. Him from wealth but me, not so much. William looked at me and said, "Hrodebert, you are assigned to the most southern regiment and in the second wave of horsemen." And, I looked at him almost angered for not being in the first wave. He looked back at me and said, "Hrodebert, do not ride that horse so fast." That was the first moment that I truly realized I might not see Penelope again.

I remembered her sweet kiss. I looked down from my vantage point. I could see the Scotsmen. They did not look like barbarians. I heard a cheer that said, "For England!" The hair on the back of my neck stood up. I had drawn my sword and as I looked at the sword in my hand, I thought, "It is not the Scotsmen, it is war that has made barbarians out of both of us."

The horses in front of me started to run. I soon realized I had passed every horse in the second wave. I had almost reached the middle of the pack to the first wave when one arrow hit my horse, *Gertie*. She did not even waver. In fact, I believe she ran even faster. I felt something hit my left side. Yet, I did not waver either. If Gertie could carry on, so could I.

Then, I struck one man, and then another and another, and another and then a second arrow hit Gertie. She went down. I fought on the ground again striking one man after another. Then, I came to realize, I was no longer fighting a war, I was protecting my horse.

The next pain I felt was sharper. There was an arrow in my upper right chest. I crawled as close to Gertie as I could get. I could feel each heave as she was breathing. I looked down to see two deep gashes in her side. I knew she could not catch her breath. I raised my sword one last time to end her pain. I knew also, I could not breathe. I closed my eyes. I said one last prayer. And, clung to the final bit of beauty I could imagine in this world. I envisioned one more, sweet kiss as I told Penelope, "Goodbye."

In the summer of 1297, about a year before, I had dreamed of raising horses. If only I could find the suitable stallion for my mare; the horses, I knew, she could and would produce. I already had a small plot of land and between horses and sheep, I knew I could make a living.

Some would say I was a bit quiet, maybe even a bit awkward. I was more comfortable among the animals than with people. Some would also say this might have sounded rude but when I met Penelope at the social, I thought she just might be the right stock for me.

When the wind blew, her hair would fly as the light glistened off her blond mane. Her laugh was cute. And, when she laughed, her eyes twinkled.

I offered what I could which was a ride on my Gertie. I will have to admit to pushing Gertie just a little harder because the faster Gertie ran the tighter Penelope held onto me.

Penelope and I were both alone and young. I was nineteen, Penelope eighteen. Neither had a family. Penelope cared for the twin boys next door and sewed. I cleared land and soon discovered a beautiful stallion belonging to the family with the twin boys. Thus, I had reason to frequently stop at the farm next door to Penelope.

Gertie was not in heat. So, my reason for stopping was definitely for Penelope. It became my custom to ride by the farm at just the time Penelope was heading home. A quarter of a mile was not far to walk but Penelope never rejected the offer to ride with me home, on Gertie. About nine months passed.

It would not be long until I met William. I also discovered that William was the illegitimate son of King Edward I. He was recruiting men for battle against Scotland.

The offer of money and a soldier's pay was appealing, allowing me to purchase lambs and more horses. I would then have something to offer Penelope.

The first night I told Penelope of my plan, she threw a bowl of soup at me. Thirty minutes later, I was asking her to marry me on my return from war.

I thought this was as good a time as any to propose as I was already on my hands and knees cleaning up the soup.

She had put a kettle of water on the fire and went into the other room. I took it as a hint to clean up the soup.

However, when Penelope returned to the room and I was kneeling on the floor, she went to the pot of warm water, brought over a rag and washed my face, cleaning the remnants of soup from my hair.

So, I asked her to marry me and she laughed. I almost got up and left. Yet, she put both of my hands in the hot water and cleaned under my fingernails. She pulled the shirt over my head and washed my chest and back. She made a sort of comment about how a husband of hers would never get into her bed after riding on a dirty, dusty, old horse all day long.

Awkward as I was, I thought she meant yes to my proposal. She said, "Tomorrow, when you come for dinner, if you try to wash up a little better before dinner, I'll try to serve the soup on the table."

It would only be about another week before I'd leave to train for war.

During the next week, I went to Penelope's nightly for dinner. On the last night before I left, she had prepared chicken and potatoes. She had the kettle of water boiling over the fire.

I took off my shirt, washed my chest and back and cleaned under my fingernails.

We ate, we laughed and we cried.

Turning to me, Penelope laughed again. She said, "Remember what I told you. No dirty, dusty horseman will lay in my bed." She finished the other half of my bath.

That next morning, she awoke in my arms. We both got up and started to dress. Neither of us quite had the words to say. As I stepped out her front door and I kissed those soft lips one last time, she would not let go of my hand. As she pulled me back into the house, I pushed her back into the house and onto her bed.

I got up and dressed, telling her not to get out of bed. I wanted to remember her just as she was.

I loaded up and straddled Gertie. Penelope did, indeed, get up and rushed to the door. She stood on the front porch, me on my horse facing her. I told her, "I love you." I turned Gertie and urged her to run away from the porch because at that moment, I feared I would get off my horse to stay with Penelope.

Three months later, Penelope heard that many men perished in the battle that day in Falkirk and that I was never returning home to her.

Lessons Learned in This Lifetime...

- In war, no one wins... not love, not man, not woman not a horse.

As was the case in those past three instances of lives, the parties involved experienced many types of conflicts and loss. You can only imagine how if they had more lives and more chances, the type 1 conflict based on information would not have occurred.

Consider that David and Ariela, Constance and Raynald, Corna, Penelope and Hrodebert were all experiences of the same souls. These souls are repeatedly living different forms of conflict; whether it was a conflict with neighbors, countries, religions, spouses or within themselves.

We learned with David and Ariela, *ahav* and *ahava*, meaning to give and true love, were the real messages or point of their story. What we now know is that conflict based on conceit, selfishness and jealousy as it was with Constance, Raynald, Corna, Penelope and Hrodebert are the opposite of *ahav* and *ahava*. Unlike Ariela and David, their lives evolved around conflict with religions, relationships and countries.

Even in the case of David there was a form of unforgiveness toward his aggressors. Thus, his seed was also replanted. You could draw a parallel to Penelope who chose not to forgive the participants in the war. Ariela was unable to complete her path and was replanted and given another chance. We must also consider that unforgiveness is in some way the opposite of *ahav* and *ahava*. And, we must assume, that taking of a life has to be one of the most negative actions by taking another's opportunity for growth and completion, regardless of the justification, for humanity cannot justify the taking of another's life.

Chapter 7
Jesus of Nazareth

We believe that there is clear evidence the existence of this man, Jesus, actually occurred in history. Other writers of the time, including Josephus, the Jewish historian, corroborate the belief of his existence. It is also apparent Jesus's life had a great influence on both history and religion. His three-year ministry as documented in the Bible is pivotal to the history of humankind. Jesus's teaching of love resonated with the people of his time. The Essenes, of which Jesus belonged, were preparing for a new messiah, a king or an enlightened one. This paralleled mainstream Jewish thought that God would send them a liberator like Moses in their past. This liberator would return the Jews back to their promised land. This time is also simultaneously important as the Romans were suppressing the Jews and expanding their empire.

We first meet Jesus in the New Testament at his birth. Later, we are reintroduced to him at the age of twelve. The New Testament suggests that Jesus was around thirty years of age when his ministry began. What happened to Jesus between the ages of thirteen and twenty-nine?

In the nineteenth and twentieth centuries, theories emerged stating Jesus had visited Kashmir, India, between the Great Himalayas and Tibet. It is written, Jesus studied Buddhist and Hindu religions at that time. There are theories of Jesus studying with the Essenes in the deserts of Judea.

There is at least some evidence according to various publications that, indeed, Jesus was learning eastern religious thought and strong Jewish heritage during those missing years.

Reincarnation was a common thread in orthodox Jewish thinking and in Hindu and Buddhist traditions. Again, the Essenes, (one of the three divisions of the Jewish faith) during that time were preparing for the next great teacher of enlightenment and the next messiah or king of the Jews. In Essene literature as documented in the Dead Sea Scrolls, the next great teacher, messiah or king could have been more than one individual.

The Pharisees believed they held the authority to interpret Jewish law. The Sadducees were under the belief they had priestly privileges as the descendants of King Solomon's Zadokite priests.

The Essenes believed their purpose was to keep the Jewish faith pure in their tradition. They did not approve of the liberal beliefs of the Sadducees and Pharisees (the other two divisions of the Jewish faith).

Jesus himself stated in the Bible, in the book of Matthew, "Elijah is John the Baptist." Some interpretation of this is that Elijah and John the Baptist are one in the same. Again, is this a direct reference to reincarnation?

John the Baptist was a strict Jew who taught we needed a cleansing of the soul. He used an outward sign of the cleansing with water or better known as *Baptism* to represent this cleansing.

In Christian thinking, the fact of Jesus allowing John the Baptist to baptize him was for all of us to follow suit and cleanse our souls. If Jesus was God, was it necessary for his soul to be cleansed? A normal Essene practice of daily bathing, eating clean food (kosher) was a way of bringing yourself closer to God. Remember, Jesus was part of and studying with the Essenes.

If Jesus is also God, how much closer does he need to be? He is God, so they said.

So, we have a man named Jesus. He is present after Lazarus's supposed death, according to the New Testament. He witnesses Lazarus's soul return to his dead body. So, either Lazarus had an NDE (near-death experience) or the soul can leave the body and return. This directly parallels the story in the New Testament of Jesus's own death, NDE or resurrection. Again, this is saying the soul can actually survive without the physical body.

According to the New Testament, Jesus the man, who at age twelve astonished the religious priests of the Jewish faith in the temple, who was absent for eighteen years, who probably studied with Tibetan and Hindu religious leaders and the most strict Jewish division, the Essenes, came forward with a message of love. This was a man who believed strictly in Mosaic law. Mosaic law is the law of the Torah, which is the first five books of the Bible. The first five books of the Bible define God's covenant with the Jewish people or man.

In the first five books of the Bible, God's disappointment in man is outlined as well as the history of man. Each case confirms that God continues to maintain his covenant even in his disappointment. In other words, God continues to love us and give us another chance after each time we disappoint God.

According to the Bible, Matthew 4:1-11, Jesus spent forty days and forty nights in the wilderness being tempted by *the Satan*. *The Satan* asked him to prove that he was God. The Bible also states that Jesus felt all temptation from *the Satan* but resisted. The Bible states that Jesus did not eat for forty days. Apparently, he drank during those forty days. In other words, he was fasting. Who wouldn't be tempted to eat during a food-free fast? He was hungry. We would all be hungry. Although Jesus said, "Man does not live by bread alone," the Bible states he resisted all temptation. The Bible does not say that Jesus *was not* tempted. Can God be tempted?

Shortly before Jesus's near-death experience or resurrection, he went to the Garden of Gethsemane close to the Mount of Olives where he prayed. Matthew 26-42, Jesus asked God to, "Let this cup pass him by." Why do you believe, if Jesus was God himself, he would ask himself this question? Why would Jesus ask such a "human" question? Jesus, like all of us, was not without fear. Fear is that primal instinct of self-preservation.

The Last Supper is where Jesus gathers those who are closest to him and asks that they remember him.

One of Jesus's last spoken words while on the cross or crux was, "My God, my God, why have you forsaken me?" Again, this was a very "human" statement from Jesus.

Did Jesus come to fulfill the law, as Christians say, or did he come to remind us of the law? And, by law, we mean, did Jesus come to remind us of the rules on how we should live?

Jesus did not come to remind us that God is a vengeful God. He came to remind us that God is a God of love. Here's a man, Jesus, trained in Buddhist and Hindu thought of becoming your best self and all within the laws of the Jewish faith to honor God by becoming your best self. It was never about punishment or vengeance. A loving God will recognize your efforts.

Jesus said the greatest commandment is to *love* one another.

Chapter 8
Paul of Tarsus

Paul was not one of the twelve apostles who traveled with Jesus. Paul (also known as Saul) was born around the same time as Jesus but in Tarsus, Turkey.

He never met Jesus, in fact, although he was considered to be one of the first generations of Christians and was often revered as the most important person after Jesus in the history of Christianity. Paul was a faithful Jew. And, early on, was known to persecute Christians. Paul's writings began approximately two to three years after the crucifixion of Jesus.

His writings were in Greek. The Dead Sea scrolls are believed to be the actual writings of the original Torah and other historical documents of the time and are written in paleo Hebrew and in Aramaic. Several of the texts are translated from Hebrew into Greek.

Paul never had access to or read the Dead Sea Scrolls. They were hidden in Qumran until the 1940s. He was a Jewish scholar from Turkey. Paul met with Peter and James in Jerusalem; they were from the original twelve apostles traveling with Jesus. Paul was the journalist, taking the story from two of the actual players.

Remember, Peter denounced Jesus three times. And, then Peter later stated that Jesus returned to him (John 21) and recommissioned him as the head of the church. Peter told Paul that many people had seen Jesus alive after his death. Peter said that five hundred people had seen Jesus after his death. James spoke and said, "I also saw Jesus after his death." Paul was building his story for his own writings. Matthew, Mark, Luke and John were books written after the letters of Paul, which are the books on the life of Jesus. The books on Jesus's life were written after Paul had sent letters out to everyone, telling them what to believe. *The New Testament stories were written after Paul sent letters out, telling people what they must believe.* The stories were written to back up what Paul had already given as the word.

The majority of the New Testament was written after Paul began writing Galatians and are written by subsequent followers. Paul is believed to have written fourteen books of the New Testament, a man who never met Jesus, and wrote from hearsay. Some would say his writings were inspired. We will say, our writings are inspired.

The book of Luke was written between AD 80 and 90 and Acts was still being revised well into the second century, AD 200s.

Paul was educated in the Jewish faith and because of the political and social unrest at the time, he believed the "Coming Messiah/Mashiach," or anointed one, would be soon.

In his lifetime, Paul had heard of Jesus; however, still persecuted those early Christians who were following Jesus.

Then, the story of Paul's conversion to Christianity at about his age of twenty-eight to thirty occurs while he is on the road to Damascus. He has a vision during his trip in which he states he talked to Jesus. Paul's story is explained in the New Testament. In his story of talking with Jesus, this is after the crucifixion of Jesus and his supposed death.

Now, apparently, talking to someone who has passed over to the spiritual realm is possible as documented by Paul. Paul in Pauline Doctrine believes Jesus is God, therefore, Paul is talking to God. Although many Christians believe God only speaks through Christ today and in the New Testament, Paul is clearly stating that he spoke with Jesus.

Paul's real issue was how to reconcile the word of God in the Old Testament with the expansion of Christianity? He had to reconcile Jews as the chosen people with the expansion of Christianity in the non-Jewish world. Thus, he had to discount the Old Testament, written by the Jews in order to allow non-Jewish persons into the Christian faith.

Why? If the Old Testament is not discounted, and by that we mean prove that it does not have as much strength as the New Testament, how will he gain the belief by the people who are not Jewish? He must argue:

1. We are not responsible for our own actions, as The Old Testament states.

2. Thus, we are only saved by the death of Jesus.

3. The old laws of the Jewish faith, stated in The Old Testament, are only a guide, for instance, on circumcision and dietary restrictions (eating kosher). Those being converted to Christianity did not have to follow the old rules.

4. So, the new rules are to love your neighbors as yourself because it was a saying by Jesus and Paul still had to concoct a moral code. This new rule would instill goodness in people just as the Ten Commandments had.

5. Paul must overcome Zionist history, which is the return of Israel to the Jews as the promised land.

6. Paul's response had to be, "Jesus is coming, soon, to create the new Zion or Heaven on Earth." This is not Israel but rather Heaven.

The importance here is the Roman Empire was expanding at an incredible rate, faster and farther than any other civilization before as is Christianity with that expansion. Why? Because the Romans insist on those who are conquered be converted to Roman Christianity. Additionally, the Old Testament's belief that we are responsible for our own actions, is also *written out* as Jesus died for our sins. Jesus was returning back to Earth soon, according to Paul, meaning no one would return to another life or incarnation as the Old Testament states.

The history continued at the fall of the Second Temple Jerusalem. The temple is representative to the Jews and all the new Christians and each time the temple was destroyed a new temple was to be built. For the new Christians, this means a new Zion or Heaven must be built because that was the basis for their conversion. The old Jews believe Jerusalem must be returned to them, the chosen, as their promised land.

The Temple was none other than a metaphor for reincarnation. How? A man with a fall or a failing in the Old Testament, literally when the Jews failed, was reborn again with a new hope.

The metaphor in Noah and the Ark is the cleansing and rebuild of the area and again in Moses's time when the Red Sea is parted and man passes through the sea only to find the other side of the sea, a rebirth and a new beginning in the promised land.

Nero's persecution of the Jews and the Christians continued. God had already intervened through Jesus, and we were saved. If we were saved, why then does our suffering continue with Nero? The book of Revelations is a story of the continued persecution of the Christians and how Jesus will return to stop the persecution.

To match the two stories, if Jesus was not returning soon, then the fact that he died and saved us, had no meaning. We all were and are still suffering and waiting.

So, in conclusion, what has Paul fashioned and what has the church continued to fashion? Paul took the story in the Old Testament of God's covenant with the Jews that he would send a great king and return their promised land, and that the Jews were responsible for losing their own promised land to a story. The story was converted to: *none of us are responsible for our own actions and that Jesus (or God) takes the blame.* And Paul's final statement is, "Accept Jesus and let him take the blame." Thus, church history and policy has been to suppress any teaching that does not support letting Jesus take the blame to the very point of stating, "If you do not let Jesus take the blame, you will go to Hell."

It appears that Paul is saying, despite God's words in Genesis after creation, *that all is not good, it is a flawed system, I am not an omnipotent and my creation is not perfect. And, as God, I'll have to take responsibility for all of your actions because of it.*

This implies a couple of different thoughts. Even though there is evidence to the contrary that God has only intervened twice that mattered, it is insinuated that God's only intervention was in creation and in taking responsibility for the failed humanity he created.

If this doesn't add enough insult to injury, God says, "if it's not my fault, you can go to Hell."

Chapter 9

The Gnostics vs.
Everybody Else

No discussions on these topics can occur without a basic introduction to the Gnostic books and Gnosticism in general.

Although the Books of Enoch are considered to be part of the Apocryphal books, they are referred to by the Gnostics as the highest books in the Pistis Sophia as we spoke of before.

Enoch lived at the time of Noah. In fact, Enoch was Noah's grandfather. Parts of the Books of Enoch were discovered with the Dead Sea Scrolls though never included in the King James Bible. The Books of Enoch have made their way into the Ethiopian Coptic Bible.

The Gnostic Books were found buried in Nag Hammadi, Egypt. These books are Coptic translations of Greek originals. The originals were destroyed during the early Christian struggle while trying to define orthodoxy, being the literal translation of the original Christian and Jewish writings.

Gnosis is defined as *knowing*. It means a mystical knowledge of spiritual things and truth. The Gnostics believed they gained secret knowledge from Jesus that he had not revealed to everyone. They gained mystical knowledge by examining how Jesus lived and his teachings.

The Gnostics had differing beliefs than traditional Christian beliefs. For instance: They believed Adam and Eve to be a story of symbolism. Adam represented the soul's lower self and Eve represented the soul's higher self. Why? Because Eve showed Adam the way to enlightenment through love which is God. Man was thought to be darkness and woman was thought to be light. Together, the two would find God through love. Light represents good and bad represents darkness.

The Gnostics believe the cleansing of the soul which the story represents as man can be cleansed by the light, which is woman and love. This cleansing of the soul brings us closer to God. Detachments from the world and material concerns and focusing on love cleanses the soul.

The Pistis Sophia is about the divine female. It is part of the excluded books of the Bible and part of the Gnostic Books. The Gnostic Books include teachings on Mary Magdalene.

Why would you suppose the Christian and Jewish beliefs differ so greatly from the Gnostic views of Eve (woman)? The orthodox Christians and Jews thought Eve as a weak, insecure woman who could not resist temptation. The cultural context of the time places women in the role of property, along with the cattle, etc. The Jewish and Christian teaching places the blame on Eve or women for the fall of man. The Gnostics believe the fall of man/woman to be the weakness of the soul.

The Gnostics believe in a cleansing of the soul in order to return to the light which is God. John the Baptist did not mean cleansing of the soul to be literal in baptism. Baptism was a symbol, somewhat Gnostic in thought, as a way to cleanse your soul or return to God. Jesus, himself, allowed John to baptize him thus acknowledging a Gnostic or mystical cleansing of the soul.

The Gnostics believe in a literal rebirth on Earth by cleansing your soul. This rebirth on Earth allows you to be closer to God. This is literally what the Christians have deemed as *born-again* by baptism. However, the Gnostics also taught reincarnation.

For the Gnostics, the soul could be cleansed over many lifetimes until it reached a level of perfection. They refer those people reaching that stage as *Perfects*. The *Perfects* literally had their final resurrection in their last life and did not have to return to Earth again because they had become one with God. This is why the Gnostics feel such an affiliation with Jesus. They believe Jesus reached the state of being *Perfect* and therefore a resurrection after death did not matter.

■　■　■　■　■　■　■　■

Back to the Books of Enoch. Was Enoch a mystic? Was Enoch an early Gnostic? The Gnostics would define Enoch and many of the other prophets as mystical. Having the ability to obtain knowledge by observation or experience with the divine. Much of the Books of Enoch was actually written in the pre-Christian Gnostic time frame.

The Gnostic Books and Enoch both spend a great amount of time discussing angels and devils/demons. These are lesser spiritual beings that interact between God and humans. This is not accepted by the Christian or Jewish church as their canonized beliefs. Yet, these stories are the stories taught by the church on the presence of good vs. evil. In fact, the Gnostics believed that humans could become angels. And Gnostic teachings are that Enoch became Metatron (Estes), the scribe of God. The parallel for the Gnostics is a human, either Enoch or Jesus, can become so good they become like an angel or holy and in union with God. That means they believe any human can become holy, or in union with God.

Job 38:4-7 states that angels were created before the Earth and witness to the creation and they shouted for joy. Angels were there ahead of man, to do God's will. The Bible states man was created in God's image. It never says that angels were. Thus, angels and man are not the same.

Now, back to the Essenes from a previous chapter. The Essenes are Biblical literalists. They believed the law should be followed to the letter. They believed their purpose to be prevention of liberal thoughts of the Torah. Interestingly enough, the Apocryphal Books of Enoch are found within the library of the Dead Sea Scrolls discovered at Qumran, home of the Essenes. Even in Qumran there is an apparent battle between Gnosticism and orthodoxy.

■　■　■　■　■　■　■　■

Did Paul of Tarsus (the supposed writer of much of the New Testament) borrow some Gnostic thought? And how was it that Paul had a vision on the road to Damascus which was believed and canonized in the Bible but Enoch's visions were ignored? Because Paul on his journey saw suddenly a light from Heaven that flashed around him. He fell to the ground and heard a voice say, "Saul, Saul, why do you persecute me?" Saul (who is called Paul) asked, "Who are you?" The voice says, "I am Jesus who you are persecuting."

Interesting, isn't it, that a Jew who was persecuting Christians in the Roman name, who had never met Jesus, has a vision of lights in Heaven and hears Jesus speaking?

The men traveling with Saul (Paul) stood there speechless. They had heard a sound but did not see anything. Paul got up from the ground and realized he was blind.

Later, Paul has to defend himself against the Roman King Agrippa with the accusation of antinomianism which means rejecting the law and arguing against moral and religious norms. In Christianity, antinomianism is one who takes the principle of salvation by faith and divine grace to the point of asserting the saved are not bound to follow moral law such as the Ten Commandments.

Again, salvation based on a theory of resurrection which saves you without regard to the law, is what Paul was claiming.

This goes along with Gnostic views. Paul's Gnostic view, as we discussed in a previous chapter, is different than the legalistic view of the law being taught by Jesus's original Twelve Apostles. This parallels the same thing happening in Qumran. The Essenes had both a Gnostic Book and were practicing a legalistic view of the law.

This battle continued even to the theologian Origen who practiced both a Gnostic view and a legalistic view of the Jewish Torah and the New Testament.

It was believed that most of the Gnostic Books were destroyed, burned or declared heresy by AD 200 by church fathers until additional books were found later in Nag Hammadi. The longest known existing group of Gnostics called the Mandaeans, is still alive and practicing in Iraq today. They are a monotheist and Gnostic religion. They respect Adam, Abel, Seth, Noah, Shem, Aram and mostly John the Baptist. The Quran describes these men as people of the book alongside of Jews and Christians. They are referred to as the Sabaeans which relates to baptism in Aramaic.

❊　❊　❊　❊　❊　❊　❊　❊

Dissension continued in the Christian world until AD 325 at the Council of Nicaea in Turkey. Three hundred Catholic bishops out of eighteen hundred bishops gathered to vote on the essence of Jesus. This took place nearly three hundred years after the crucifixion of Jesus. The question to be voted upon was whether Jesus was begotten or created. The result of the vote was that Jesus *always was.* This became the literal orthodox position.

AD 367, Bishop Athanasius of the Coptic Orthodox Church, the assistant Bishop to the Roman Emperor during the Council of Nicaea, listed the sixty-six books for the Bible, agreed upon as supporting the literal orthodox position. The sixty-six books were not voted upon.

Then another Gnostic vision occurs from the angel Gabriel. He appears to Mohamed.

The Gnostics always speak of enlightenment. If the lost years of Jesus included him studying in Hindu and Buddhist regions where enlightenment is taught and if Jesus is the enlightened one the Essenes awaited, if Moses had visions, Enoch had visions, Jesus had visions, Paul had visions, and Mohamed had visions and then we have the last of the canonized books of the Bible, the Book of Revelations (the most cryptic, Gnostic, mystical book of the Bible) is it any wonder that this becomes confusing? Exactly who and what do we decide to believe?

Part II

O

Omega

The End is Not the End, This is the Omega

Chapter 10

Atonement

The Jewish belief in Atonement is based on a process. The process means there is a transgression that must be forgiven, pardoned or corrected.

Some Hebrew literature calls the land of She'ol the area of Atonement.

In Judaism, the theory is on redemption; God redeeming the people of Israel from their exile or slavery thus, a final freedom. The celebration of Yom Kippur is the redemption of celebrating Atonement. Atonement is believed to be a requirement of Mosaic Law or the Ancient Law of the Hebrews.

None of the above beliefs differ from the theory of reincarnation. Reincarnation is the belief we live, die, atone and come back to another life to correct a transgression. This is Mosaic Law. Paul of Tarsus stated that Mosaic Law did not matter.

Paul said that Mosaic Law was created for sinners yet we are all still sinners. There is another conflict in the order. Paul said the new Christians did not have to heed the Mosaic Law.

Paul taught that Israel alone had received the Mosaic Law and that Gentiles were excluded from the law as was the Christian church which he taught was the body of Christ.

Paul wrote most of the letters of Galatians to correct the peoples' misguided thoughts to confirm that Christians did not have to live under the Mosaic Law but under the administration of grace not law.

In AD 51 at a Council of Jerusalem, Peter recalls the story of Cornelius in Acts 10, to Paul of Tarsus. Paul is arguing that he himself had spoken with Jesus. Peter questions how it was possible for Paul to speak with Jesus when, after Jesus, God would talk to no one. Peter revealed that his friend Cornelius had also spoken with God when an angel appeared to him. The angel came to Cornelius who was not a Jew. His message was to tell Cornelius he was a good man and had been called by God to do God's work. Cornelius asked Peter if he will enter his house although he is not a Jew. This was during the historical time when Peter was banned from eating with Cornelius due to the Kosher Law. When Cornelius kneeled at Peter's feet, he realized his friend has had a religious experience and spoke with God without being Jewish or following Mosaic Law.

Paul states that Jesus told him to ignore the Mosaic Law for all Christians. Here they are at the Council of Jerusalem. Paul and Peter are telling conflicting stories about the law. Paul says that you are saved by grace alone through Jesus and Peter states that your actions are the deciding factor along with your faith. Both parties are attempting to persuade their argument. Then, Peter recalls his friend Cornelius. He changes his story to convince the others to follow Paul, using Cornelius as his reason.

This was the beginning of the disbelief in reincarnation. Paul and Peter's story together was now, we are saved by Jesus for our actions. Jesus was coming back in the near future for our final days of Atonement.

This insinuated we had to be saved at that precise moment! Literally, from that moment on, everything was immediate and there was no room for redemption, atonement or another chance. No one would have another life, no one would go to purgatory, there were no chances for redemption through prayer because the end was right in that moment.

If the end was in that exact moment, why have two thousand years passed? And...we are still waiting.

———

Atonement is not about the exact moment. Atonement is a process and a reconciliation of the karmic position of your soul. It is not a pronouncement of guilt but rather a discussion. In any discussion there must be two or more participants. It must be about learning how to make positive choices. It has to be about mercy, grace and self-responsibility.

Atonement must occur in God's realm and with God present. For in the earthly realm, it is always too easy to focus on things from our own perspective. So, the concept of She'ol, Purgatory or the land of Atonement is a time between lives when God can touch us and we can understand God's mercy. We may receive some limited choices after self-evaluation on the lessons we still need to master and the karma we must still overcome. God will guide us to the correct choices. We will be reincarnated and our life as well as our choices will be laid out in front of us. Atonement is simply a reconciliation with God.

Chapter 11
History of Hell

Some of the first recorded histories of the dead occurred in ancient Egypt. It was associated with the kings or pharaohs and has become known as the myth of the God Osiris.

It involves Osiris who dies, goes into the land of the dead and is raised again as the new pharaoh. Thus, all pharaohs after that were believed to die and return as Gods. They were passing through the land of the dead. This happened three thousand years before Jesus.

Perhaps there are similarities to the death of Jesus, King of the Jews and the belief he traveled through the land of the dead and returned as the Christians' God.

There is a history of passing through the land of the dead and returning which is reincarnation or resurrection.

Naraka is the Hindu, Buddhist and Jain belief of Hell or its equivalent. In Hindu, it is the abode of Yama, the lesser God of death. It has been described as being south of the Universe or beneath the Earth. Messengers from Yama are called Yamadutas. They carry you from living to death. Yama then weighs your virtues and vices. From there, you are either sent to Svarga or

Naraka. Svarga is the Hindu name for Heaven. Both Svarga or Naraka are generally a place you stay temporarily until you are reborn to your next life or possibly from Svarga you may go on to a higher plane.

Naraka (or Niraya) in Buddhism is relayed as Hell or Purgatory in English. This is somewhat similar to Diyu, the Chinese mythology of Hell. They differ from the Christian *Hell* belief in two ways. If sent to Naraka it is not a punishment or divine judgement. And, the time you spend in Naraka is not eternal. It is normally arduously long in years.

In comparison, the Hebrews believe in She'ol as the place where the dead souls reside to atone. She'ol is sometimes referred to as the land of atonement. Yom Kippur is actually the Jewish holiday of atonement. Not unlike the Christian thought, during Yom Kippur the Jews are literally praying for their past-over souls to achieve a higher plane and reach their atonement.

Also, in Hebrew history, their great city is Jerusalem. Jerusalem was built on a hill. The valley next to Jerusalem was called Gehenna. During the Jewish historical time of the Judges, Gehenna was where the illegitimate children of the kings and judges were put to death by burning. It was also where the sewer system of Jerusalem drained. Excrement, animal remains, all liquid waste, emptied from Jerusalem into Gehenna. In Jewish lore, it became known as the land of the wicked, of burning fires, and of death. Picture a place, below where you live, where fires burn constantly with spontaneous combustion, with odors from excrement, death and killing and a despicable place to end your existence. This is also the area where Nero persecuted Jews and Christians, putting them to death.

Understand, in the time of Nero, the Second Temple of Jerusalem was again destroyed although Jerusalem was considered the promised land, or Heaven on Earth. Jerusalem sits higher than Gehenna, the wicked land.

Back to Naraka. A soul would be born in Naraka again, due to an accumulation of their karma or actions and remain until the karmic debt was satisfied. Naraka closely parallels the Christian concept of Purgatory.

The next most highly educated and developed civilization precommon era are the Greeks. The Greeks had a complex view on God as being several entities with Zeus being the highest God. Zeus was believed to live in the highest spot known as Olympus with twelve other higher Gods.

The lesser Gods, in Greek mythology, were believed to be the actual offspring of the higher Gods. One of the lesser Gods was called Hades, known as the God of the underworld. If Olympus was above Earth and the land of Hades was below Earth, we can realize the "fallen" connotation of going to Hell or death in the lower or under-area. The God Hades also owned an incredible beast with three heads of a dog.

When you compare this knowledge to the Hindu belief of three great Gods (in one) with one most powerful God Brahman, and the system of many smaller, personal Gods who reach out to humankind to the belief of the Greeks where there are greater and lesser Gods, the similarities are not far from Judaism, Christianity and Islam where there is a main God and lesser beings referred to as Angels. Thus, a fallen Angel then, becoming the head of the Christian *Hell* is easy to theorize.

Let's go back to the Osiris myth. When the early pharaohs received their God name, they were referred to as Horus. The Horus is a mythical man with the head of a falcon. This ties directly into the Egyptian myth of the Phoenix, which is the bird that lives out its entire life, burns and rises again as a new bird, a new Phoenix again...the story of reincarnation.

The Horus name for many of the Egyptian pharaohs is cobra or snake, as seen in the Egyptian Pharaoh, Djet. He was from the first dynasty of the Egyptian pharaohs 3000 BC and all other pharaohs from that dynasty returned as a God named cobra or snake.

In Hinduism, they focus on mainly one kind of snake, the King Cobra, referred to as the Nagas. The cobra is believed to be a great devotee to the Gods. The snake in Hinduism represents rebirth, death and immortality. Their association with the snake symbolizes being fearless and eternal, like reincarnation.

Thus, the first reference in the Bible to the snake draws on history of the snake being a lesser God associated with God and the Bible. It further states in the Book of Job that God assigned one of the Angels to play the role of the Satan, meaning the adversary.

Job is a wealthy, good, God-fearing man. The Angel assigned to be his adversary discusses with God how easy it is to be a good man when you have wealth as in Job's case. The Angel says, "Let me make it not so easy on Job, and see how he reacts."

Job becomes poor and tormented as a result of the Angel's interaction. God says to the Angel, "See, Job is still as good man." After he completes his appointment as the Satan, he returns to his normal Angelic activity.

In Greek mythology, Medusa has sharp fangs and live snakes for hair. Additionally, in Greek mythology, snakes were regularly regarded as the guardians of the underworld and were considered messengers between the world and the lower world because of their living in cracks in the ground. It was believed that looking on the face of Medusa would turn you to stone. Medusa was a woman not a God.

All of the history leading up to the time of Jesus, with all of the civilized societies, has led to a culture of various definitions of *Hell*, various definitions of lesser beings serving God and association with the evil snake/cobra which is associated with sin and death and the underworld.

Although the role of the Satan (adversary) was technically assigned by God, the thought of this lesser God, Angel, offspring of God is the one who is fallen, believing to reside in a lower world.

The most educated group, the Greeks, pre-Jesus's time, were slowly infusing their Hellenistic beliefs upon the Hebrews, whether they lived in Jerusalem or Alexandria, Egypt.

The Greek beliefs or Hellenistic views included mythology and philosophers such as Plato and Aristotle which influenced Jews such as Philo, the great Jewish philosopher. Philo harmonized Jewish scripture and the Torah with Greek philosophy.

The Hebrews had also been arriving in India since the time of King Solomon. King Solomon was responsible for trade with India.

You can now see throughout history, up to that point, how the Greeks, Egyptians, Indians, and now the Hebrews became intertwined in their religious beliefs on God, Hell, Angels, the Satan, death and karma.

It is obvious, at this moment in time, how the next great empire, the Romans, had the capability of spreading throughout the world at such a rapid pace. They helped to spread this somewhat convoluted belief system of God, Hell, Angels, the Satan, death and karma throughout the entire western civilization.

The Romans already had their own concept based on *the good dead* going to Elysium and *the evil dead* going to Tartarus. Both were ruled by Pluto, the God. Pluto and Hades were believed to be one in the same.

The Book of Revelations, in the Bible, speaking about the beast with seven heads is making reference again to a beast in a land like Hades, and the dog with three heads. The book also references a new Zion, which is a reference to a new Jerusalem, because of the destruction of the Temple, the second one, yet again. Nero was the destroyer of the second Temple. Nero was the emperor persecuting the Jews and Christians and burning them in Gehenna.

Could Nero be the beast, or the dog like Hades?

The Book of Revelations also talked about the old serpent described as the dragon. The serpent is depicted as a red, seven-headed dragon with horns.

If we put all of this together historically, we have a story of a lesser God, acting symbolically like a man on Earth, who destroyed the promised land or Zion, at the time of the Hebrew and early Christians believing a Messiah was coming to create a new Zion or Heaven.

There is then a great Roman expansion, making it believable there is a good place to go once we die and a bad place to go when we have died. There is a lesser God or being, believed to have some control over where we go, once we die and that place is associated with beasts, serpents, fire, suffering and death.

The Roman Empire expands throughout the entire western world. Most of the writings were done in the educated world in Hebrew, Aramaic and Greek. Thus, the terms, Gehenna, She'ol and Hades predominate.

The Roman Empire expands into Europe along with the Roman Catholic church. Much of the Old Testament is in Hebrew. Much of the New Testament is in both Hebrew and Greek, therefore, in about the third century, Origen the scholar, had much to do with the translation of the already written text into Greek from the New Testament. Origen is from Alexandria, Egypt. He uses many versions of the translations to form a consistency in the writing. He uses the text of a scroll, he discovered himself in the valley of the Jordan, which much resembles one of the Dead Sea Scrolls. In AD 382, Pope Damascus commissioned Jerome, the leading Biblical scholar of the time. Jerome declares there are so many corrupt versions of the Bible thus the church has now stated themselves, their records are not accurate and, therefore, a new Latin version needs to be developed. Damascus also believes that a Latin version is necessary for the Roman populace since the majority of Romans cannot read anything but Latin.

As the Romans expanded so quickly into many areas, Christian-Europe could only speak German, French, Anglo-Saxon, Italian, Spanish, etc.... Latin was then saved for those who were learned. Thus, the newly translated Bible became used and owned by priests, predominantly. It became a policy that translating into any vulgar language would be discouraged. Vulgar language was anything other than Latin.

From then on, there was a relatively high demand for translations of the Bible into other languages. The first English version was translated by John Wycliffe, in 1376. During that time, Wycliffe could not find reason in scripture for any authority for a pope, in the translated Bible.

Pope Gregory XI considered Wycliffe a heretic. He persecuted him and placed him in jail. However, Gregory died and Wycliffe was released from jail.

Two other men decided they were both to be the next pope. Gregory XII of Rome and Benedict XIII of Avignon were fighting over their authority and, thus, forgot about John Wycliffe. They eventually agreed and decided there could only be one pope in Rome.

Martin V takes the role of pope. He had been a cardinal but not a priest. Therefore, they rushed him through the stages of deacon, priest, bishop and then to immediate pope.

John Wycliffe, who had since died, was exhumed and burned for heresy under the new pope, Martin V.

So, let's turn back the clock 1,400 years when we had Nero burning Christians in the valley of Gehenna. During that time, King James I needed a legitimate English Bible. He was responsible for commissioning the King James Bible. The actual translation was by William Tyndale and fifty-four other biblical scholars. He continued to modify his translation for ten years as to match the current biblical opinion. Tyndale later became a leading figure in the Protestant Reformation.

Interestingly enough, the scholars of the time drew from old Norse and Germanic mythology in their beliefs of religion. Norse and Germanic mythology had a God called Hela. Hela was over the underworld. Hela was the Norse Goddess of Death. The Norse (Viking Descendants) also had a concept of Heaven called Vahalla. It was known as the place *the good dead go.*

The King James Bible translated the words She'ol, Hades and Gehenna to **Hell**, which is based on a pagan religion's beliefs practiced by Vikings.

Interestingly, King James I's wife was of Danish/Viking descent.

And, *Hell*, was basically and categorically a ditch outside of Jerusalem which was translated into a place we most fear at the end of our existence. Though, historically, if you read all religious beliefs, *Hell* appears to be much closer to Purgatory or a land of Atonement.

Chapter 12
Grace

A common thought is that we are either a cosmic accident or a creation by the action of God. We exist not by something earned or deserved. Our existence occurs at the moment of creation. Again, this is something that occurs without our deserving or earning it.

Divine grace is a theological term present in many religions, per Wikipedia. It has been defined as a divine influence which operates in humans to regenerate and sanctify, to inspire virtuous thought and to impart strength to endure trial and temptation. It is an individual virtue or excellence of divine origin.

Again, in Wikipedia, in western Christian theology, *grace* is the love and mercy given to us by God because God desires us to have it not necessarily because we have done anything to earn it.

Our existence is proof of divine influence or *grace*.

Before our actual existence and before our karmic debt and before our sins, we were given life/*grace*.

Remember, religious thought is that we have an existence before the physical body on Earth. That existence is immortal. Does this mean our creation is evidence of having a divine influence operating in humans that allows us to regenerate and/or become sanctified from the beginning? Does this also mean that *grace* is based on love and mercy?

Grace must be based on our created potential. *Grace*, apparently, is not based on our actions, sins or karmic debt.

However, sins, actions or karmic debt are what we must endure and overcome through trial and temptation during existence.

In none of the above does it state, we are not responsible for our actions. It merely states that our existence is because of *grace* and that our potential is to live up to the excellence of our divine origin. Our divine origin is created from love and mercy.

Part of our creation, again, is created with the ability to choose with free will and the ability to make our own decisions. Thus, we must make choices, allowing us to overcome and create a life based on love and mercy. Otherwise, we literally choose a life or lives incongruous with our creation.

When we think of the life of Jesus, we are reminded of his belief in living lives with love and mercy. *Grace* already exists before our lives, during our lives and after our lives.

The life of Jesus is a reminder of how to make appropriate choices; again, choices based on love and mercy. Jesus forgave his executioners, Jesus invited all persons to his table, Jesus walked with those who denied him, Jesus suffered all indecencies and continued to be loving and merciful, thus, the example of a virtuous life. He turned the other cheek. He did not condemn. He did not judge.

He preached that the humble, not the conceited would inherit the everlasting connection with God. (Matthew 5:3, 2 Timothy 3:1-5)

He preached about selfishness, not to be concerned about our own good but for the good of others. (Philippians 2:3, 1 Corinthian 10:24)

He preached about not being jealous and coveting. (James 4:2-3, Ecclesiastes 4:4)

He preached about forgiving others, ourselves and not judging others. (Mark 11:25, Luke 23:34, James 4:11)

He preached that God's love was for everyone, therefore, we should love everyone including ourselves. (1 Corinthians 13:4-5, Matthew 22:37-39)

Jesus apparently believed we are responsible for our own actions based on the above scripture. He tells over and over again about controlling our actions, what to do and what not to do. In fact, Jesus never used the word *grace* anywhere in his teachings.

We have talked about Paul, a Jew from Tarsus. It is, indeed, Paul from Tarsus who introduced *grace* in the Bible. He mentioned it many times in regard to the Jewish social covenant of responsibility and reciprocity for generosity. The word *grace or* charis literally means favor, *grace*, gracious, thankful, acceptable, gratitude, liberality and bounty. In other accounts Paul uses the word *charisma*, meaning in Hebrew a gift, free gift or spiritual gift. Paul also uses *charizomai*, translated to mean give, forgive, deliver, gift up, grant, freely give or bestow.

These words imply a relationship with God based on an understanding of respect, and reciprocity with God. Reciprocity, meaning the practice of exchanging things with others for mutual benefit; basically, privileges granted.

Grace, the way the human understands it in Christianity has become one-sided; coming from God only. However, Paul uses it as an exchange between man and God.

Presumably, our interpretation is based upon the fact that we have nothing to offer God. However, that implies that God wants nothing from us.

Humans should not assume to understand God's intentions. However, as Paul taught in the Bible, there is some expectation of reciprocity of God's love.

Thus, Jesus is a Jew who preached that Hebrew law was the way to God and Jesus is the example. Paul taught that Jesus was fulfilling the law and *grace* is the reciprocity deserved to God. Only God gives us *grace*.

Therefore, Jesus and Paul of Tarsus both had expectations in their teachings of reaction from us in regard to how to act and why we act.

All of our actions require free choice.

The religion of Buddhists, Hindus and Jains speak of the responsibility for our actions as humans. Therefore, they believe we take responsibility for our choices/actions. Is this any different than the teachings of Jesus and Paul from Tarsus?

Grace provides us the following framework: We exist because of God's love and mercy. As a reciprocal requirement, God expects us to choose to live by the rules and choose to love God. The two cannot be separated.

It is all in the intention. Do we choose to be involved in our church because it flatters us, or do we choose to be involved in our church because we are honoring God?

Do we make choices that are based on love and mercy, because this is what God expects? This is our reciprocity with God.

Thomas Merton was a well-known Catholic-Trappist Monk and writer who was inspired by Zen Buddhism and the exploration of his higher self. He was one of the most prolific Christian mystics and writers of the last century. He died in 1968, but before his death he wrote seventy books on spirituality, social justice and pacifism. He was a strong proponent of interfaith understanding and often discussed Zen Buddhism as a way to explore his own Christian beliefs.

His books discussed nondualism and dualism as a Christian theory of growth. Nondualism teaches that a person is responsible for their own actions and choices and cannot rectify this themselves versus dualism where God's forgiveness of the failings of man comes through Jesus. He discussed that, as a Catholic, he could only believe the two must come together. His knowledge was gained through mystical experiences such as meditation.

Thomas Merton wrote that, "Every moment and every event of every man's life on Earth, plants something in his soul. The beginning of love is to let those we love be perfectly themselves and not to twist them to fit our own image. Otherwise, we love only our reflection we see in them. In the last analysis, the individual person is responsible for living his own life and for finding himself. If he persists in shifting his responsibility to someone else, he fails to find out the meaning of his own existence."

Not unlike us, Thomas Merton stated that we must live both as Jesus taught and as Paul of Tarsus as well.

So, literally, it is both works and *grace*.

Chapter 13
Karma

Karma is a Sanskrit word meaning action. (Sanskrit is an ancient Indo-European language of India.) We are all responsible for our own actions. We cannot expect to blame others for our choices or expect others to take the blame for our actions.

For those of us who need a Bible scripture to confirm these words: Job 4:8, Those who plow evil and those who sow trouble, reap it. Proverbs 11:27, Who ever seeks good, finds favor but evil comes to one who searches for it. Proverbs 26:27, Whoever digs a pit will fall into it. If someone rolls a stone, it will roll back on them. Psalms 7:16, The trouble they cause, recoils on them. Their violence comes down on their own heads. Galatians 6:7, A man reaps what he sowed.

What is the great law of all religions? The Golden Rule.

Buddhism says, "Hurt not others with that which pains yourself."

Christianity, "Do unto others as you would have them do unto you."

Hinduism, "Treat others as you would yourself be treated."

Islam, "Do unto all men, as you would wish to have done unto you."

Judaism, "What you yourself hate, do to no man."

Native Americans, "Live in harmony, for we are all related."

The Sacred Earth, "Do as you will, as long as you harm no one."

The law of karma refers to the law of cause and effect. However, it is more importantly associated with the intention, motivation or choice that affects the outcome or the result. If we are motivated by greed, hatred, conceit, selfishness and jealousy, we are planting those seeds. If we act out of generosity and *love*, we are creating those seeds.

Again, it is the motivation or choice that affects our karma. Inherent in our choices is that the mind is powerful enough to bring about results that change us that cause our evolution. If we are unaware of what motivates our minds, we can actually adversely affect our karma. So, being in contact with yourself, you create more positive karma in your future. The law of karma can be understood in two different ways. It can be experiencing the cause and effect over an extended period of time but it also can be thought of as affecting your current state. When your mind is positive and loving, and has an openness and loving effect, some of the effects of karma are immediate and can actually overcome your past karma.

Karma is not about punishment as insinuated in religion. It's about learning compassion. It's about forgiveness and appreciation of potential in others as well as in ourselves. Saying five *Hail Marys* and praying for our own forgiveness will not erase karma. Praying for and forgiving another is key. Causing karma is against God's plan. What YOU do, does matter.

If you are doing something motivated out of greed or hatred, it may bring karma in the future which is negative. We need to be aware of how karma works. Karma is God's *love* directing us to make loving choices that will not only affect our current karma but our karma in the future.

Buddhism has erased the thought of "I" in their belief. "I" is usually one based on the self. However, the Buddhist's belief in love of everything, is correct yet missing the connection to the creation of God which starts with the infusion of *love* into everything.

Decisions based only on yourself at the negative expense of others affects your karma. So, if we cultivate loving kindness, we start to cultivate *love* and kindness for ourselves. When we anger, we bring upon anger, when we *love*, we bring upon *love.*

We can use this analogy of dropping a stone in water, creating the ripple effect. The ripple effect of positive karma on us and others causes positive outcomes. The negative ripple effect of karma causes a negative outcome.

When balancing the positive and the negative karma, you get back to *love.* You have gone through all the stages, learning all the lessons. We are created with *love,* we literally fall, thinking only of ourselves. Then we grow and our soul returns to not only *love* but to a much greater *love.*

The concept of living every side of every life and understanding another's life is really the basis, and with that understanding, comes the learning of compassion.

Karma is not just fixing your wrongs, it's about improving your "rights" which lead to not only a better self but also a greater *love* of everyone including yourself.

Does Karma act like a magnet? In some ways, yes. It draws you to the situations and the people you need to address. There is a very delicate balance between what we believe is fate and what we think is choice.

The persons we are drawn to is not by accident. However, how we connect with them may be affected by our choices. You may interact with them as a friend. You may interact with them as a boss. You may interact with them as a spouse. You may interact with them as a parent or child. For having children is a choice we make.

You can make a choice to not interact with that soul at all. The interaction may be brief or lifelong. Again, it is all by our own choices. The extensions of that choice may be more than one life. For instance, you may choose to be spouses more than once. You may choose to be a spouse and another time, their child. This allows you several lifetimes to conquer your karma with them, making good choices.

Every interaction, every day of our lives has a moment of brief interaction with every other human on Earth. Consider the interaction with the sales clerk in the grocery store. That moment of interchange could be brief; however, if that brief moment is creating karma such as with rudeness or lack of compassion, and you never again have a chance to repair the karma you created, you have now started the next chain of karma which could ultimately cause you to return with that grocery store clerk again somehow, somewhere.

That store clerk could someday be your enemy in a battle, or your spouse. Ouch! Was your devaluing of that person really worth it? Thus, your karma has become a magnet to your soul.

Does this mean the karma you created with the store clerk is unfixable? No. Consider though, if you have learned from that experience and treated the next clerk with respect and dignity, that next clerk may be patient with another shopper. And, in some way on some path, not understood by you, that clerk and the next shopper may interact with the spouse or friend of the original clerk, and, in some way that *love* may be returned. That ripple effect may reach the first clerk and, in essence, balance your karma as well. The Domino theory. Never consider your karma being too late or extensive to repair.

Perhaps you own a beautiful, kind, loving, white husky dog with blue eyes, a gentle spirit and a playful demeanor who graced your life with joy and happiness. Your dog infused your life with energy. One day, your beloved dog who loved to run like the wind and be free, somehow released himself from your property, finding your neighbor's property as well as their own dog. Naturally, the two dogs played/tussled to find their superiority, causing the neighbor to believe his own dog was in jeopardy. Without fully considering the situation and with fear, the neighbor carelessly shot your beautifully spirited family member, taking his life forever.

The loss of your energy could have caused willfulness and retaliation toward your neighbor, creating more karma. Instead you chose to place your energy and love into a memorable eulogy of your lost dog as a story to be published. Focusing *love* allowed no additional karma to be created. Your neighbor has his karma to be dealt with. However, no retaliation toward your neighbor has certainly stopped karma on your part; in fact, the forgiveness toward your neighbor may have started the ripple effect, potentially balancing his karma.

We are not defined by our karma. We are defined by our actions related to the karma. Karma is a state of being. It does not have to define who you are. It defines who you were at that moment in your actions. That karma still requires an action or a choice in reparation. *Love* or *forgiveness* is required to overcome it. *Love* and *forgiveness* are not just a feeling, they require action. We often speak of karma as an *eye for an eye*; however, *an eye for an eye* creates more karma. But, consider, if you injure someone's eye you should be willing to buy him glasses or bandage his eye. That is the action.

The injured party also needs to consider whether his actions started the injury to his eye, and if so, an action is required on his part. How can he repair the damage, aka karma? He must also consider forgiveness, releasing his injurer from karma.

Let's consider human history. In the beginning, in the Bible, in fact ever since Adam and Eve, six thousand years ago, karma began. Their children Cain and Abel created karma with murder. Cain killed his brother Abel. Was this Cain's karma or was this a karma related to his parents? Is there an ancestral karma? Yes. Is the birth of Jesus and the development of Christianity related to antisemitism in the Holocaust 1941-1945, when the Jews were persecuted and murdered? How does this relate to the persecution of the Christians by the Roman King Nero AD 64–AD 313, during the edict of Milan where the Roman Emperor Constantine legalized the Christian religion? Think about it.

Is the enslavement of the Egyptians of the Hebrews in 1450 BC, Moses's people, the mitigating cause of the Holocaust? Think about it.

Is the Roman expansion throughout Palestine and then Europe 800 BC–AD 400, a cause of the Holocaust? It is all of history which leads the human race to be the very cause of all developments.

Is it a war based on power, family against family as it is in the Tudor and Lancaster families during the War of the Roses in England 1455 to 1485? Is this any different than Cain and Abel? Power and murder prevailed in all instances.

What karma was caused by the Crusades of which there were nine, AD 1095–AD 1492, where Christians of Europe attempted to retake possession of the Holy Lands from the Muslims?

If you are a Christian, it is your treatment of non-Christians that causes karma rather than you being a Christian. If you are a Muslim, it's not your belief of the Quran that causes the karma but rather your belief that nonbelievers are wrong. It's the judgement and treatment that causes karmic debt and your **conceit** in believing you are right and others are wrong.

So, if you are Jewish, you cannot retaliate because of the Holocaust; only **love** and **forgiveness** can overcome that karma.

In 1492 is when the Muslim religion was driven from Spain, Portugal and all of the Iberian Peninsula taken by the Christian religion. Then ask yourself, what did the Iberian Peninsula have to do with the Holy Lands? Isn't it just power and murder and karma?

What about the debate between church and state? This again is another great divide and by who's doing? The one gaining power. Now, we have state against state (country against country) and church against church. And, speaking of two sides, if there are two or more political parties involved in state or national matters, must we divide them as well? Can they agree to have differences of opinions and not crucify each other for their differences? If there is a winner or a loser, karma is created. Compromise and compassion should be of the most importance, not who is right and who is wrong.

Slavery in Egypt, three thousand years ago, was when the pharaohs enslaved their own people, then the pharaohs enslaved the Hebrew people, and now we enslave based on sex, creed, religion, race, nationality and any/all differences, including economic; a complete circle again. The pharaohs enslaved the poor, and again five thousand years later, we are still enslaving the poor. For what? Power and *conceit.*

If you lived on a plantation in the old south where slaves were used, even if you treated the slaves well, did you enjoy the benefit of their enslavement? This was *selfishness* and all about you. Anytime you benefit at the expense of others because you believe your way of life is deserving, you create karma of your own to overcome. So, if your people were enslaved, whatever their nationality, race, or religion, only *love* and *forgiveness* can overcome karma.

Let's bring this into present day. As a boss, do you exploit your employees for your own benefit? If you are the husband or wife, do you exploit your spouse for your benefit, and is the relationship fifty-fifty? Are the decisions you make about your benefit or theirs? How does that effect the ripple/domino trickling of the world? Again, consider, is this choice made out of *love **and** forgiveness or selfishness, jealousy or conceit?*

Are you creating karma or correcting it?

And, who exactly holds the responsibility for the state of the world? Humankind of which we are all part. In other words, we all have karma related to the outcome and situation of the world. And, for those of you who say, "We weren't there and didn't cause any of this," we say, "What actions have you performed to correct the wrongs?"

Because, a choice of inaction still affects your karma!

Do we have responsibility to correct the karma of the past? This plays into race, prejudice, nationalism and all the well-known "isms" including sexism. Do we have *conceit* related to who we are or who we were?

We are responsible for not passing our karma onto our children. Isn't being prejudiced just another way of passing our karma onto our children? Isn't sexual abuse and other abuse just another way of passing our thoughts/karma onto our children? It requires an action to prevent our children from seeing our ways. We are perpetuating more karma. We are growing more karma for ourselves and our children and whomever they interact with.

Christmas karma is passed onto our children. What we believe is forced upon our little, impressionable children. You may believe you are starting a tradition of giving; however, you are actually starting a tradition of taking. If your intention is to teach the act of giving, why buy gifts for Jesus that are not given? Jesus would want you to give of yourself to those in need, those who are hungry, those who have no family. Giving of yourself does not mean going to the store to buy presents. Teach your children to donate their time to shelters as a family; find a needy individual and donate clothes, food and help of any kind but not presents and material wealth. It's not about who gives or gets the best gift or the most of their time but rather the act of giving of yourself. It is not a competition. There is no winner or loser unless karma is created.

Revel in the family tradition of giving, do not revel in the family tradition of taking. And giving does not only occur one day a year. It's a complete mind-set. Giving of yourself continually means in all areas, not just on December 25 or the eight days of Hanukkah.

Giving gifts on birthdays teaches each individual child that they are somehow more special for being born. Having a birthday cake is one thing, buying them a car or sending them on a trip is ridiculous…just because they were born? Give that wasted money to someone in need. We were born for a reason, and the reason was not to create more karma. The reason is to *love* which overcomes karma.

We do not give in *love* only on special days. It must be given daily with everyone, otherwise we become *selfish* with our *love*. Otherwise, it appears we are giving it only for some special reason and that is what we are teaching our children.

We are teaching our children that **LOVE** costs something! In all reality, **LOVE** is the only thing that does not cost karma.

We should not teach our children to consume without consideration. It teaches our children that immediate gratification is of importance. What are the consequences for consuming without consideration of the future, which is the karmic outcome?

This includes how we treat our precious resources and the planet on which we live. It is the most direct way we pass our karma onto our children without realization. We litter, cause more than our share of trash, smoke, burn emissions, destroy trees, waste water, pollute water and make extinct our animals and plants.

If we eat gluttonously, consuming more than we need, do not be surprised when one day, we or our children find ourselves hungry or in need. It's karma. We reap what we sow.

If we re-create this world as a dump, should we be surprised when it resembles a dump? If we eat in excess, should we be surprised when our entire country is full of overweight, unhealthy persons, never missing a meal?

If we drive nature to extinction, along with ourselves, we will no longer have an opportunity to remedy our karma.

Yes, there is an individual karma for each of us. However, we must consider the presence of group karma also. The summation of all karma within a group as we mentioned earlier—nationalists, religions, racists etc. should also be evaluated. Our mere participation in the group creates negative karma for yourself. Let's take it one step farther. Is there karma based on our membership in the human race? Thus, when we experience a disaster, a pandemic, a war or potentially the extinction of the planet, are we not part of this human karma?

One of the greatest examples of group karma is the pandemic of the coronavirus. Did we individually and as a group come together? Or, did we hoard selfishly and protect ourselves conceitedly? Were we jealous of others who successfully returned to everyday life afterward when perhaps we did not? The battle for the future is not today. It's every day. The slightest thought that we would consider this a battle created karma: us against them. In any conflict when we assume there is a winner and a loser, karma is created.

Let's go back to the original point...the ripple effect. We are each responsible for our own actions and how it affects group karma.

––––––

Does God's love and mercy or grace, along with our created potential, make karma more likely? So, consider if God loves you, how many times would God allow you to make your own choice and yet still forgive your poor ones?

Isn't the choice to choose any religion an attempt to choose the correct path to God? Remember, even Thomas Merton, the "Buddhist-Catholic" monk, stated there was a dualist reality, which is that we are saved by grace and saved by our choices to change our actions. Because, even the acceptance of God's grace is our choice to choose God's *love.*

Since humankind has the potential to grow and evolve, what human can actually have the right to say that God's grace can stop? Even if you are an atheist and choose a humanitarian approach to life, what you are really saying is that your ideology is based on human potential. It's not all about church.

If God created us, there must be a purpose. And, if that purpose is everlasting life with God, then God must believe in our human potential to fulfill that purpose. However, if we observe the reality of the world, we see that bad things happen. Thus, it must be part of our human potential to overcome those said, bad things. And, isn't that what karma is really all about; which is overcoming and fulfilling our potential?

Is one life enough to fulfill our reciprocity with God?

Where does the cycle of life end and begin? Where does the cycle of the soul end and begin? How long could it take to balance? And, if we have human potential what happens at the end of life?

What if we have not balanced? What if we have not forgiven? From a religious perspective, what if we have sinned? At the end of our life, we are doomed, according to religion.

Even religion has tried to explain that there is some sort of human potential to overcome and grow after death. For example, purgatory which we discussed previously, is where you remain to contemplate your actions. Most religions suggest we pray for our deceased *loved* ones. Why? Because, if the human potential does not exist after death then what happens after death is irrelevant, correct?

The reality becomes, there must be even based on religious thought, the potential in the human soul that transcends death.

The human potential that transcends death must be the ability to overcome our actions.

And, what is the definition of karma? The sum of our actions.

The Sum of our actions...

And...when WWII began, the shit hit the fan!

War and conflict, as we've adamantly said, is one of the most crucial reasons for jealousy, conceit, selfishness and unforgiveness to cause karmic debt.

––––––––

Remember, as we have already discussed, the seed is replanted many times during our journeys. How does the battle of David and Ariela influence the lives of Katie and Johnny?

Katie and Johnny were born in the late 1930s to a normal middle-class family in the midwestern United States. They had loving parents. The family lived in a slightly older, multiple level home with a dark-wood, three-story staircase. Post-Depression, they were certainly not well off. However, the family was rich in other ways.

A loving wife and husband existed in this household. Their children laughed and played, content with happiness and love. The brother and sister were inseparable. Katie was six years old and Johnny was four. For some reason, Katie always referred to her younger brother as J.J. which stood for Jonathon Jackson. Jonathon was for his grandfather and Jackson was for his father.

During Christmas time in the year of 1941, Katie and Johnny's father Jackson had completed his flight training in the United States Air Force. Jackson and his wife Rose decorated a lovely, live Christmas tree that sat in the front window of their living room. It was complete with presents, a single doll for Katie and a toy gun for Johnny.

Katie and Johnny were not aware that their father was leaving for duty after Christmas nor were they aware that this would be their last family Christmas.

Three days after Christmas they watched their father walk down the front steps dressed in his crisp, pressed uniform and jump into the back of what they believed was a green bus. They each held their mother's hand as she cried.

Rose could not understand how WWI and, in fact, how all wars, had led to this day.

We should ask how had retaliation in the Treaty of Versailles against Germany, stripping the Germans of military strength, national identity and portions of their land caused a new form of German Nationalism? How did the increase in Japanese and Italian military, the fear of Communism and Socialism in Germany all contribute to the responsive nationalism of our country? How did Great Britain gaining a false sense of security in Germany, also lead to this point? The United States had gone through a financial crisis in the Great Depression. This provided a cause for the United States to join in.

As Germany tried to develop a new nationalism, they also tried to develop a unified front which would both control and motivate their citizens. They used age-old methods of control. They invoked race, religion, affluence and fear. So, within their borders they undertook an action not that much different than the Crusades and the Inquisition against the Jewish people.

Anyone who was not Hitler's chosen people could be persecuted. And any country who did not want to be persecuted, would have to choose Hitler's side. We've seen this throughout history over and over again all in the name of religion, nationalism, racism and classism.

Was this war a result of all wars? Was Nero's persecution of the Jews and then the Christians, the destruction of Jerusalem, the expansion of the Roman Empire just one more step toward the next war?

Rose stood on the front steps of her home crying and wondering why at a time of Christmas when the lessons should have been to give and to love, she was losing her husband and her children's father to war.

Interestingly enough, at the time of the Jewish Holocaust, unbeknown to Rose, she was holding the hands of David and Ariela whose paleo-Hebrew teachings were to give or *ahav* and truly love or *ahava*.

Jackson was deployed in an Air Force plane flying missions and bombing over Germany. Lives were lost indiscriminately with many innocent children in the crossfire.

Rose and the children wrote many letters to Jackson during the following year. Most of their letters were never answered.

They did receive one letter back, however. In it, Jackson wrote, "The horror of war has overcome me. I fear for my very soul. In fact, I fear for all of our souls. War is so Godless. I love you and the children with what little heart I have left."

The months passed as another Christmas approached. Rose purchased another Christmas tree even if it was much smaller. She decorated the tree and placed an orange under the tree for each child. There would be no Christmas cookies that year. As she decorated the tree, children would still be children.

Katie and Johnny played on the top level of the three-story staircase. As they played, Johnny believed Katie to be falling from the stairs as he reached out his hand to help her. He started to fall. Katie also reached out to help her brother. Rose heard Katie yell out, "J.J.!"

Both children fell to their deaths that Christmas Eve of 1942.

Jackson returned from war with no victory to be celebrated. He clung to the last thread of love remaining in his heart which was his wife Rose and she to him.

They soon had another child, a daughter, they named Carla. Jackson, Rose and Carla never decorated another Christmas tree until the mornings of Christmas.

Whose karma was this related to? Was it Jackson's for taking the lives of innocent children? Or does this karma belong to all of us? All war is related to conceit, selfishness, unforgiveness and jealousy. Or does this stem back to Ariela and David's daughter Kahlia, stealing the son of Miriam and Covid, whose son had been replanted as Jackson? *It was the sum of all of our human actions.*

Lessons learned in this lifetime...

- We are always too quick to lay blame, for the blame lies with all of us.

Chapter 14
Our Actions
or Intentions

An *emotion is* a response to stimuli. All responses are either learned or based on nature. A basic response is hunger. Hunger is not really taught, it is experienced. Some of how we respond to hunger can be learned however. On the lowest level, hunger is a feeling that you need nourishment. So, if you don't eat, on the basic level, you hunger and die.

On a slightly higher level, we learn that not being hungry equals comfort. We then learn to tie comfort to those who feed us. And, we also learn that food can give pleasure as in a chocolate addiction or caffeine addiction. Being hungry becomes something much more than a basic need. The next step could be like any addiction, to hide, as in eating excessively to avoid connections, stress or just plain gluttony.

It, therefore, is not the action of *eating* that causes karma but rather the reason we choose to eat. One is a learned response, and one is based on nature's facts.

Now, let's go one step farther. If someone stops you from eating or there is a reason you are unable to eat, like due to lack of food or lack of resources, we again evoke a natural response related to nature's survival of the fittest. Thus, causing us to compete for food.

A learned response to this could be our cooperation in the hopes of producing more food, as in a community garden or a group hunt for meat. We can then work together or against each other. Therefore, we're creating an intention of either cooperation or competition.

In competition, it is rarely a draw. There is a winner and there is a loser. At its lowest level there is an instinct for survival but at its higher learned level there is a judgement. The thought corresponding with that judgement is that *I am more worthy of survival.* This higher, learned level is the beginning of *conceit.* This is much different than needing food because your body requires it to satisfy the hunger.

You now believe you deserve the comfort of food, pleasure and satisfaction, over another. You may even hoard food as was the case during the COVID-19 outbreak. Now, we have moved ourselves from *conceit* to *selfishness.* Remember, a winner and a loser always emerge. Having enough which is all we really require becomes then, never enough. We classify ourselves as the loser causing our emotion to change from *selfishness* to *jealousy.*

What if we now are angered and retaliate? Isn't it quite interesting how anger can *eat* at you? You retaliate because you believe you have been wronged. You blame someone else when, in fact, you competed and did not cooperate. If you had only forgiven, the anger would not have *consumed* you.

It actually comes down to this very simple point: Is your action or intention based on competition or is it based on cooperation? Cooperation is based on equality and respect or simply based on a famous quote: "Love others as you would yourself." Those things that are *loving* and forgiving in intention and action bring about positive karma. Those things that are *conceited, selfish, jealous* or *unforgiving* bring about negative karma or karmic debt.

Chapter 15

Do We Reincarnate
or Not?

W hat is déjà vu? It is described as the feeling of already having experienced the present situation. According to howstuffworks.com, about sixty percent of us have claimed to experience this feeling at least once in our lifetime.

So, we've either been in this situation before, we feel we have met someone before or we have been in this place before. However, we have not met them before, this is our first visit to this place and we believe we have never encountered this situation before. Scientists will argue this is poor memory or some kind of electrical malfunction of the brain.

Could you imagine the possibility of this being an actual situation memory from a previous time not in this life? Could you imagine the possibility of having met this person not in this life but in a previous life? Could you also imagine being in this exact place, not during this life but yet in another previous lifetime?

How do you explain a child prodigy? Interestingly enough, most past-life therapists believe the children up until the ages of three and four remember past lives. Is it then surprising that they may remember past talents? A child prodigy is defined as a person under the age of ten who can meaningfully perform at an adult expert level.

Frederick Chopin published his first composition at the age of seven. Why was he playing the piano at such a high level by age six?

Another well-known Freddie, Mercury that is, started to master and play the piano at age seven. He formed his first band at age twelve.

Akiane Kramarik, from rural Illinois, outside Chicago, realized at age four her interest in painting. She first appeared on a popular talk show at age ten, telling the host her talent came from God. By the age of twenty-one, her childhood paintings were selling for hundreds of thousands of dollars each. One of her most popular paintings was of Jesus which she completed at age eight. Now, at the age of twenty-one, she has noticed a maturing of her technique. She now admits to painting *soul-scapes* which is her artistic interpretation of the soul's journey.

William James Sidis was born in 1898 as an American child prodigy with exceptional mathematical and linguistic skills. He was conversant in twenty-five languages and entered Harvard at the age of eleven. His book published in 1920 was *Animate and the Inanimate* about the existence of dark matter, entropy and the origin of life in the context of thermodynamics.

Perhaps Sidis had a previous life as Galileo or Isaac Newton. His hypotheses at a young age certainly drew an understanding of advanced math and science as theorized by Galileo and Newton. We may never know until we die, but we should consider thinking about the possibility.

An article in the *Chicago Tribune*, June 21, 1995, stated that Dr. Brian Weiss, a well-known, past-life regression hypnotist and psychiatrist, was able to successfully hypnotize and regress 75 percent or greater of his patients.

David Spiegel, a professor of psychiatry at Stanford University School of Medicine, has research on hypnotism. In his research, using MRI, he has confirmed that there is a change in the brain in 75 percent of the population during hypnosis. Also, during his studies, he found that around 25 percent of his patients were extremely difficult to hypnotize.

Dr. Weiss, as written in his books and as quoted on Wikipedia, has regressed over four thousand patients.

The Newton Institute was founded by Dr. Michael Newton, PhD. His first book, *Journey of Souls*, was published in 1994, sharing his experiences with twenty-nine of his seven thousand clients, exploring their afterlives and lives between lives. Dr. Newton was a hypnotherapist and held his doctorate in counseling psychology. *Journey of Souls* tells how his patients, while in deep hypnosis, described what happened to them between their former reincarnations on Earth. They also gave vivid details about how it felt to die, who met them at the moment of their death, what the spiritual realm was like, what we do as souls, where we go and why we decide to come back in another body.

Alex Heigl, *People* magazine and *Entertainment Weekly* associate editor, underwent Past-Life Regression with a therapist Ann Barham, according to an article he wrote on September 17, 2017. The article stated that he had been skeptical and did not believe he could be hypnotized. Yet, he relived a past life as a Depression Era man living with his family in California. His job was working for the WPA program. His experience was somewhat unsure, he describes, however, he found the people during his hypnosis familiar and the situation similar in regard to present-day issues he was facing.

The *New York Times* published an article, August 27, 2010. In one of his past lives, a doctor Paul DeBell explained his belief of being a caveman in a previous life. Dr. DeBell is a Cornell-trained psychiatrist who was living in New York during this publication. He went on to say he believed himself to also have been a Tibetan monk and a German who would not betray his Jewish neighbors during the Holocaust.

According to Gaia.com, an estimated one million people have accessed past-life memories most commonly through guided regression hypnotherapy.

On a guest post by Coletta Long, PhD, a clinical psychologist specializing in regression therapy, she states to having regressed thousands of persons over the past sixty years. Dr. Long is also an ordained Unity minister, author, teacher and lecturer. She also states her reasoning for regressing patients is to help them discover themselves and to better understand their true nature and purpose on this planet.

An article in *Psychology Today*, October 14, 2012, by Alex Lickerman, MD, stated that the belief in reincarnation ranges between 12–44 percent depending on the country. In the United States of America, the number was 20 percent. He stated that psychiatrist Ian Stevenson had conducted more than 2,500 case studies, over 40 years, on children who remembered past lives. He methodically documented each child's statement and then identified the deceased person the child had identified with. He verified the facts of the deceased person's life that matched each child's memory. At the same time, he started matching birthmarks and birth defects on the patients to wounds and scars on the deceased. He verified these by medical records such as autopsy photographs. Dr. Stevenson's book on this documentation is *Children Who Remember Previous Lives*.

It is a well-known psychiatric principle, hypnosis can allow a person to recall suppressed memories in their subconscious, such as childhood trauma. Thus, why are memories from the subconscious on a past life so hard to believe and therefore discounted?

NDEs are near-death experiences. Dr. Eben Alexander, a Harvard-trained neurosurgeon, discussed in his book, *Proof of Heaven*, which is his own Near-Death Experience.

Summary from Wikipedia: Being a scientist, Eben Alexander never practiced religious belief and did not believe that near-death experiences could occur. Alexander thought of near-death experiences as an illusion that felt real but did not actually occur. One late night in the year 2008, Alexander woke up with a severe headache and did not think anything of it. In the moment, Alexander said to his wife that he's a doctor and he knew nothing seriously was wrong with him. The next morning, he was rushed to the hospital, where he spent seven days in a meningitis-induced coma. Once he had woken up from his coma, Alexander was told that he had suffered from a very rare form of meningitis, bacterial meningitis, and his recovery was a miracle. During the seven days of his coma, Alexander claims that he experienced the afterlife and he met and spoke with God. This afterlife experience proved to Alexander that consciousness is autonomous from the brain. After this experience, Alexander now began to believe in life after death, religion and the soul. This journey is revolutionary considering it happened to someone who did not believe in any religion or life after death. He is now teaching people that it is through this belief in religion, the soul and the afterlife that true health can be attained.

Dr. Alexander and thousands of others have delivered much the same story. They describe themselves floating above their body, and they spend time in a beautiful, otherworldly realm. They talk about meeting angels and passed over loved ones. They feel a sense of connectedness to all of creation, and they feel a loving presence that some have called God. Almost always, they claim to have reluctantly returned to their own body.

The importance of Dr. Alexander is that, as a neurosurgeon, he was able to study his own medical chart and determine his brain had completely shut down and, consequently, he did not believe it was a hallucination caused by brain activity.

According to the web, the following religions claim to have believers in reincarnation:

- Hinduism

- Buddhism

- Judaism

- Christianity

- Islam

- Sikhism

- Jainism

The majority of these religions with a strong belief in reincarnation are of eastern and Indian origination.

Certainly, it is a major tenet in the Jewish Kabbalah as it is, in early Gnostic Christian works. The Druze are an Islamic-sect believing in reincarnation.

Abraham, Moses, Enoch, Solomon, Jesus, Cornelius, Mary of Nazareth, Mohamed, Joan of Arc, the children of Fatima and Paul from Tarsus all claim to have spoken with God, angels, and/or those who had died and we don't hesitate to believe them. If you believe Jesus heard the last word from God, remember, Paul from Tarsus was after Jesus, Mohamed was after Jesus, Cornelius was after Jesus, Joan of Arc was after Jesus and the innocent children from Fatima heard from Mary, after Jesus.

Then, why do we discard the possibility that Sylvia Brown, John Edward, Edgar Cayce, Jean Dixon, James Van Praagh, The Long Island Medium, Allison DuBois, or even Shamans of the

Native American nation have the ability to speak with God, angels, Spirit Guides or passed-over loved ones? Whether it's inspiration, revelation, faith, fact or fiction…you decide.

Chapter 16
Good vs. Evil

Early Egyptian religion was the belief that all things were based on your position or station in life. So, a pharaoh could return to a life on Earth as a king or could return to the afterlife as a God, due to his position as a pharaoh.

Zoroastrianism is a religion supposedly with an origination prior to the religions of Islam and Judaism. It has a monotheist belief, meaning the belief in one God. It has one of the earliest religious traditions of involving good and evil. Geographically, this religion existed in the areas that would become Islamic and Jewish. The Zoroastrians are considered to have had the earliest thoughts of good versus evil and the source of the beliefs of good and evil in Judaism, Islamic and Christian religions.

The early Books of Enoch, which were not included in the King James Bible, were included in the scrolls of the Essenes which we now refer to as the Dead Sea Scrolls. The Books of Enoch were considered apocryphal, meaning they were secret books under the guardianship of hierophants and initiated priests. They were never meant for the common people to read.

Reading the Books of Enoch, one will find them historical. They look at this period of history retrospectively, introspectively and prophetically. They are a source frequently quoted but not canonized or included in the King James Bible. However, it is a canonized book in the Ethiopian Orthodox Coptic Bible. They describe in story form the fall of man, relating it to a fallen angel or being. Again, these are stories that compel people to have belief in a fallen angel. The fallen angel is believed to be responsible for the downfall of man. It is the offspring of the fallen angel that brings condemnation to the world. Literally, these stories blame the fall of man or original sin on fallen angels marrying human women and their offspring becoming evil or fallen humans also.

The *"story"* is giving credit to the fallen angels who are having offspring, who are, therefore, becoming fallen angels, versus fallen humans developing fallen offspring. We are responsible for our children's actions, thus this is just another explanation of how evil develops. The King James Bible blames the first evil actions on Eve for tempting Adam and, therefore, their children become evil. It was assumed in the translation of the Books of Enoch, Enoch himself agreed with the *"story."* But, do we really know that? After all, it was written one thousand years later and translated.

Enoch is talking to all of God's angels. They are telling him that the fallen ones return to Earth and marry women, carrying evil to the women and thus their children. This becomes interpreted as fallen angels marrying women.

The fallen angel story differs greatly from the story of Adam and Eve who we are all familiar with from Genesis in the King James Bible. However, the problem with the Books of Enoch are that Enoch lived one thousand years before the book was actually written down in about 200 BC, as was the story of Adam and Eve which was told and probably written in about 700 BC. The first written evidence in the Silver Scrolls (first evidence of the Hebrew-written Bible) was discovered about that time.

Included in the Books of Enoch are his visions of Heaven and astrology which include discussions on geology, ethnology, astronomy and theogony. His thoughts are both prophetic and psychic.

Take into thought that the Zoroastrian writings dated from 600–700 BC about the same time as the earliest evidence of the Hebrew Bible which included the Book of Genesis and also, at that time, the writings of Enoch are discovered. Genesis also includes part of the story of Enoch's grandson, Noah. Thus, all three appear to be the earliest discussions on the creation of evil.

So, why were the Books of Enoch not chosen to become part of the King James Bible?

Is it not yet interesting to us that portions of the Books of Enoch were found among the Dead Sea Scrolls?

The Books of Enoch are held in the highest esteem and quoted in the Pistis Sophia, the Zoharand and in the Midrashim. The Books of Enoch are also quoted by Origen, the so-called founder of the Christian theology and Clement of Alexandria, a Christian theologian and philosopher.

Pistis Sophia, remember, is a Gnostic text, found in 1773 (A book never included in the King James Bible) which includes Jesus after his resurrection. The Gnostics were mystics somewhat in the same vein as the Kabbalists. They are believed to have predated Christianity and had similar beliefs as Judaism and Christianity. The Gnostics with their Greek influence, began as polytheists and gradually changed to a monotheist view in that there was a spark of God in all of us. They believed the root of all evil to be based in the material world. Even the Jewish-early-Christian theologian Origen, said to be the father of Christian thought, agreed with the Gnostics that Earth was the highest plane of HELL. They believed that self-knowledge was the path to salvation which is having your own light in connection with the light of God. To the Gnostics, Jesus's resurrection is of no particular significance except as a symbol of Jesus reaching his human potential. Thus, Jesus became one with God or a child of God which was what all Gnostics hope for.

Zoharand or Zoharic literature is foundation work in which the Kabbalah (the foundation of mystical religious interpretations within Judaism) is based. Midrash is Jewish biblical interpretation.

The dichotomy of good and evil begins in the Jewish way of thinking. Inside a body, a person breathes a soul. Inside that body of Jewish practice breathes an inner wisdom, the soul of Judaism. This is called Kabbalah. Kabbalah actually means *receiving* as in wisdom.

In Kabbalah belief, good and evil originated in the *Adam and Eve* story when man ate from the Tree of Knowledge. According to the story, as Adam and Eve ate from the Tree of Knowledge, they began to take on God's role as judge. They began to decide what was deemed good and evil. A healthy apple that is bright and red would normally be considered good. However, a rotted apple might be considered bad or of no good. However, the rotted apple falls to the ground and fertilizes the seed. Both were created by God and, therefore, both are good, and both serve their purpose.

It's a matter of perspective. It depends on what your purpose is for the rotted apple. The rotted apple has value which means it also has purpose and potential.

In Kabbalah, it is said that the realm of judgement was never meant to be man's realm. When you take on the role of judge as to what is good and evil, it changes your perspective. Again, that is where eating from the Tree of Knowledge was the beginning of the struggle of man. If I choose to judge the apple, I can also judge my fellow man/woman, which Adam did in blaming Eve.

Rather than seeing from a perspective of up/down, right/left, or any descriptors of position, man chose to judge on value. The only true value is when one is more loving, which brings us closer to God, the light.

Why, as men/women do we continue to twist the human experience by playing God? Making judgements, casting them in categories of only good and evil, seems to be prevalent. We must learn to move past this cycle of only good versus evil which has dominated us since the beginning.

In mystical Kabbalah, it is believed that God continues to try to reach us even today! We must listen to God and only God rather than listening to our own judgements.

The best approach to finding our way back to the Garden of Eden, Utopia and nonjudgement is by relinquishing our views of good versus evil.

The Hindu approach to good versus evil is clearly identified. Good or *divinity* is represented by purity, light, balance, immortality, order, virtue and last but not least, selflessness. Evil is represented by impurity, darkness, imbalance, chaos, sinful conduct and most important, selfishness. The basic criteria to distinguish good versus evil in Hinduism is *intention*. Selfish intentions are always evil and selfless intentions are always good. Selflessly giving of yourself to God and others is the direct path to righteousness. Retrospectively, if you are serving yourself, you are on a sinful path, per Hindu belief.

Good karma leads to peace, happiness and liberation. Bad karma understandably leads to suffering, rebirth (replanting) and downfall.

Your choices lead your destiny and lives to either your bad or good karma.

In Hindu, each person is a part of the whole. Realizing this, since God represents light and good, making yourself good brings you closer to being part of God as opposed to not part of the whole or the darkness.

According to Buddhism, evil is whatever harms or obstructs the causes for happiness in this life, a better rebirth, or liberation from death and rebirth, and from a full awakening.

The right behaviors and thoughts alleviate personal pain and suffering according to Buddhism.

Buddhist thoughts are not about dualism of good versus evil. Hatred, attachments/greed and ignorance cause pain and suffering and, therefore, are considered bad.

Not focusing on the bad things will bring the good things such as kindness, compassion, joy and equanimity.

The American Indians, Iroquois to be specific, have their own beliefs concerning good and evil. A goddess has a daughter in their story. It appears to be similar to the Adam and Eve story in theory in that they have a good and bad son. The story changes however. The good boy treats his mother with respect, affection and love. The bad boy is evil and difficult to handle. His name is Flint. Apparently, he was impatiently waiting to be born using his sharp, flint-like head to cut himself out of his mother. His mother dies during the process.

The evil son is jealous. He watches the good son create trees and fruit and clean rivers. He creates hurricanes, tornadoes, massive storms and everything that can destroy all beautiful things.

Eventually, the two face each other in battle leaving the evil son imprisoned underground.

In most Native American religions, which can be monotheist or polytheist (believing in one God or several) God, nature and mankind are all part of spirituality. They are not separate. Almost all of their ceremonies are based on returning nature back to its natural state.

They believe nature to be good and what man destroys in nature, as evil.

The Quran, the most sacred book of the Islams, believed to be God's word, dictated by the angel Gabriel, has a basic theology related to evil and suffering. Its basic moral concepts include a *notion of sharr* which is an Arabic word for bad or evil. In the

Quran the meaning of the term sharr is that which man creates for himself. This sounds like what we would call karma.

The Quran says that humankind, through its own volition, acts in a way that is not in accordance with the divine plan. This is the Quran's way of attempting to explain that evil is not created by God but rather by man himself.

The Quran at least places blame where blame is due which is in the hands of man himself and not on an evil angel.

The second category related to suffering in the Quran is corresponding our anguish with a trial or a test. Suffering is meant to be a necessary component of life in order to grow and advance on our spiritual journey. The Quran states, *"It is literally part of the fruit of the creational tree."*

Much of Islam is interpreted by Sufi mysticism or in other words by mystical interpretation. The mystical interpretation by Rumi, the famous poet of the thirteenth century, states that *the only reason the gardener plants the tree is for the sake of the fruit, thus man is the goal of the creation.* Thus, Rumi postulates that *closeness to God is related to the positive impact of trials and tribulations on man's spiritual development. And, man is responsible to live in accordance with his inner nature and recognize that actualizing of his potential is possible.*

From Rumi's perspective, *the most important phase of a man's spiritual development is to get to know oneself.*

Man tends to forget his divine origin and occupies himself with worldly attainment, Rumi says. *You will be faced with adversity and suffering of your own accord. In other words, trials and tribulations of your own accord lead you to self-purification. This frees you from material attachments and the inclination of your own ego.*

So, impatiently enduring suffering as well as trusting in God and in the overall goodness of his creation, man will be able to overcome the anguish and move up the spiritual ladder to reach nearness with God, states Rumi.

On Rumi's mystical path, love of God plays a real role in our spiritual growth. And, adversity sets us on a spiritual journey. On this journey, we must learn to exercise patience, trust and love God and realize the potential of our inner nature, purifying our soul to reach perfection.

Should we use the term "evil" in our moral, political and spiritual discourse and thinking, or is evil an old or empty concept which should be interpreted correctly?

It seems that, to be evil, an action must be wrong. We tend to believe that evil actions must be connected in an appropriate way to significant harm. It is universally accepted that to perform an evil action a person must be morally responsible for what he/she does.

Perhaps the human body is evil while the human soul is good and must be freed from the body through strict adherence to limiting ourselves of conceit, selfishness and jealousy.

The religious need stems from the psychological need for group belonging, together with a need for certainty and meaning. There appears to be a strong impulse in human beings to define ourselves, whether it's as a Christian, a Muslim, a socialist, an American, a Republican, or as a fan of sports. This need is closely connected to the impulse to be part of a group, to feel that you belong, and share the same beliefs and principles as others. And these impulses work together with the need for certainty—the feeling that you "know," that you possess the truth, that you are right and others are wrong. At times our behavior is changed by this need to belong.

The fact that other people have different beliefs is a challenge, since it implies the possibility that their own beliefs may not be true. They need to convince other people that they're wrong to prove to themselves that they are correct.

"Spiritual" religion is very different from religious dogma. It promotes the higher attributes of human nature, and creates a sense of the sacred and sublime. "Spiritually religious" individuals don't feel animosity to other religious groups—actually, they are happy to research other beliefs, and may even go to other groups' temples and services. Their attitude is that different religions are best for different people, and that all religions are different expressions of the same essential truths.

The Greek Philosopher Plato (428-348 BC): He thought that man is bestowed with the knowledge of good and evil before coming here to Earth. The knowledge existed in his/her soul but during the period between their creation and their birth, they forgot most of the things. These forgotten things can be recollected either by education or through meditation on nature. Experiences help in recollecting the forgotten. All good and evil is innate in man. To Plato, the life of reason and good behavior is a happy life. Good itself is happiness and the soul's paradise. It is its own reward.

The Greek Philosopher Aristotle (384–322 BC): If man uses his reason and other capabilities properly, he can attain self-realization after which he hardly needs any measure for good and evil. The position of self-realization is sufficient for his guidance. Aristotle also considered reason and nature to be sufficient for human guidance. He said that goodness is in harmony with nature and its principles have been set by reason which a wise man can easily find.

The Jewish-Egyptian Philosopher Philo (50–30 BC): Philo thought that the spiritual part of man, his mind or soul, is the seat of good, and his body, the material part, is the seat of evil. Consequently, when the soul is incorporated in the body it suffers a fall from divine perfection and becomes predisposed to evil. Thus, the goal of man is freedom from matter and a return to God who is perfect goodness.

The Christian Theologian Thomas Aquinas (AD 1227–1274): He believed that the goodness or evil of a particular action depended upon the aim or purpose of the doer. According to him, good is that which is done, with good intention and with the knowledge that the results would be good. He said that God has created all things, including man, for good. To achieve goodness is the highest good, and the greatest good for man is to realize God's purpose in the creation of man. For Aquinas, evil is the negation of good. Where there is no good, there is evil. For him, evil is the absence of good. All things created by a good-God aim at goodness. When an object fails to achieve good results, evil comes into being.

The French Philosopher Descartes (AD 1596–1650): He regarded God to be the perfect good who, therefore, could not be the creator of evil. The power gifted by God to man to distinguish truth from falsehood is not complete. Man goes astray due to the pressure of his desires and sentiments. Due to lack of accurate judgement, he fails to distinguish between good and evil, and treads the wrong path by mistake. Error lies not in God's action but in ours, and this is due to our poor judgement which is based on insufficient knowledge.

※　※　※　※　※　※　※　※

Footprints on the Sands of Time...

What once began as a simple story of *ahav* and *ahava* between David and Ariela then became a conflict. The conflict escalated to all forms of conceit, selfishness, jealousy and unforgiveness in the late 1700s in North Carolina.

This is a time between the War of Independence and the Civil War. We were a nation created under *God*. Supposedly, we had freed ourselves from tyranny, all forms of injustice, the English control and believed we were all created equally.

Yet, a woman and land were both owned. And, a black man and a horse were of equal property. Somehow, we still claimed to believe that we were all created equally; apparently, some more equal than others.

We were well on our way to being a nation of haves and have nots. Why, at a time of peace, does man continue to search for the conflict? Just four simple words can answer the question: conceit, selfishness, jealousy and unforgiveness.

William Tolliver was accused of murdering his wife's brother in 1811, in Ashe County, North Carolina. George Reeves Jr., brother of Susannah (Sukey) Reeves Tolliver was, according to William, attempting to steal his horse. The trial took place in Wilkes County for fear of a lynch mob in Ashe County.

Susannah had shared with her husband William the details of her childhood and her sexual abuse at the hand of her brother, George.

This same abusive brother, George, was a tax collector for the county and had been on their property that day and had seen Susannah. He disclosed his reasons for being there as relating to their back taxes. Susannah assumed her husband's motive to be related to her abuse.

William's defense was based on the fact that he supposedly did not recognize his brother-in-law and feared robbery of his livestock.

One of their neighbors, State Senator David Edwards Jr. had been the procurer of the bill related to the value of horses as owned property. The value of a horse was equal to the value of a slave according to Senator Edwards. This gave an owner the right to defend their property by any means including murder.

Senator Edwards had been called to court by William's defender, Robert Henry of Buncombe. His testimony was necessary to justify the killing of William's offender and brother-in-law.

William was concerned with his wife's possible testimony. He feared she would accuse him of killing her brother not because of theft but because of the incest he had inflicted on her during her life. Williams believed his wife's testimony would not have the same evidential affect as the senator's testimony. After all, the value of a woman was nothing compared to the value of a prestigious man's testimony or a horse.

Susannah was unaware of the conversation that had transpired that fatal evening between her husband and her brother. William Tolliver had been discovered one day in a compromising situation with another woman by his brother-in-law, George. George had held William's transgressions over his head during the conversation that evening, just as William had made George aware of his knowledge of the incestual relationship between he and his sisters.

George Jr. had been belittled by his father his entire life. William was a successful rancher and farmer. This being so close to the War of Independence where taxation was looked upon so negatively, George as a tax collector was considered no better than the *crown of England* we had replaced. Thus, the irony here was that the senator who approved of the taxes was respected yet the one who had to collect the taxes was not; again, a position of power over another individual.

Senator Edwards Jr. and Susannah Tolliver became acquainted during the weeks of the trial. Both were in attendance every day.

Senator Edwards was married to Elizabeth Andrews having eleven children together. She had been sickly for most of their married days and homebound.

George Reeves Jr.'s wife was the widow Jane Osborn Reeves and also in attendance in the courtroom daily.

Jane Reeves was, in all actuality, relieved by the murder of her husband. Jane believed she had married below her station. She also believed herself to be a good, God-fearing woman but did not believe her husband to be. His lack of passion for Jane was unacceptable to her ego.

Most days in the courtroom, Jane, David and Susannah sat side by side during the proceedings. Jane learned of David's wife's habitual illness and now finding herself in a position without financial means, offered to care for David's wife and their eleven children. David accepted.

Jane began to notice the attentiveness of David to Susannah. With her sights already set on David with his position and stature in the community, her animosity grew stronger against Susannah and the attention David showed to her.

It became important to Jane that Susannah's husband be acquitted so she would not be available to Senator Edwards. She could see them growing closer as the days passed by.

Jane was aware her brother-in-law William had been having an affair with her friend, another Susan. She was also aware from her husband that he, too, knew of the transgression. There were now two reasons that Jane wanted Susannah to disappear. If Susannah testified to the truth her husband would be convicted and would leave Susannah available to Senator Edwards. If he was not convicted, would he leave his wife for the other Susan still leaving Susannah Tolliver available for David Edwards Jr.?

Jane had an agenda. She needed to rid the situation of Susannah Tolliver one way or the other. She concocted a plan. It would have to involve her brother-in-law William and her friend, the other Susan, in order for it to work. Susannah would have to disappear and the other Susan would have to assume Susannah Tolliver's identity but somewhere other than here where people would not know the truth. If William Tolliver went to prison, the new Susan posing as his wife, could sell his property as his wife, and using his wealth, begin a new life elsewhere on his release from prison, freeing Jane to proceed with a life with David Edwards Jr., the senator.

Jane befriended Susannah Tolliver in the initial stages of her plan. She brought an offering of tea to the courtroom every day for both Susannah and David. David drank his tea black. Susannah preferred her tea with sugar. Jane disguised the poisonous plant, nightshade, as sugar and added it unsuspiciously on Susannah's request.

As the days went on, Susannah appeared pale and tired. After four days, Susannah was gravely ill, noticeable to both Jane and David. Jane suggested to Susannah that the trial was taking a toll and she very much required rest and a change of scenery. She offered to take Susannah to the ocean for rest and relaxation. The trial was recessed during the weekend.

Unbeknown to Susannah, Jane, along with her friend the other Susan, had plans to escort her far away from the courtroom and her life. They drove a horse-driven carriage with Susannah as their captive traveler as far as Raleigh, North Carolina, before Susannah became too ill to travel any further.

Once Jane and Susan reached Raleigh that day, Susannah was visibly more ill. They stopped at a small, two-story boarding house. They checked into a room and escorted Susannah up the back stairway. It required both of them to drag Susannah to the room. Susannah noticed, during this time, a ring on the hand of the other Susan. The ring looked mysteriously familiar like the ring she had known to be worn on the hand of William's mother. The thoughts lingering in Susannah's altered mind were simply, "I wonder how she got William's mother's ring?"

Jane and Susan helped Susannah to the bed. Realizing that Susannah was near death, they offered her what was meant to appear as a remedy for her illness when, in fact, it was one last large dose of nightshade meant to end her existence. Susannah attempted to drink the tea in desperation.

Jane and Susan somewhat in fear for what they had done, searched Susannah's belongings for all signs of identification. Susan pulled the wedding ring off of her lover's wife's hand and placed it on the fourth finger of her own left hand. William had divulged to Susan that the ring was inscribed with Susannah's name in the band.

Susan actually thought that if William ever accidentally called her Susan, she would say that it was short for Susannah and have proof in the band.

Jane and Susan left the boarding house, and Susannah to die.

Susannah, now realizing that they had stolen her wedding ring, also realized that something was wrong. She fought her way to the bedroom door, found her way to the landing of the stairs and fell down the steps to her death.

The boarding house owners found her body an hour and a half later. They had no idea who Susannah was and her murderers were now long gone.

The trial continued. Susannah had not appeared for days. When David questioned Jane on the whereabouts of Susannah, Jane's response was that Susannah became hysterical in Durham, North Carolina, and that she had left by stagecoach for the coast.

Senator Edwards did testify at the trial. Because of this testimony, the court felt Susannah's testimony was unnecessary and thus not missed. William's defender had argued that Susannah could not testify for or against her husband with her interests in conflict.

William had been previously found guilty of killing a man for another supposed horse theft. He had been incarcerated for three years and branded on his left thumb with an M for murderer. This had taken place before Senator Edwards's' bill had passed.

This time, although acquitted for manslaughter, he was actually imprisoned for three months for recklessly shooting a firearm. Even though the court found him guilty for the crime, they were uncertain as to why William had not recognized his wife's brother. He got away with it.

For the remainder of the trial, David Edwards Jr. had wondered about the whereabouts of Susannah Tolliver. However, correspondence along with their wishes to sell, did come from the new Susannah Tolliver to the sellers of their real estate, thus, the Tolliver farm was, indeed, sold. David heard about of the sale and wondered why Susannah had never returned.

William Tolliver and his new Susannah Tolliver relocated after his imprisonment to Indiana, some said, along with his two boys. The history records show a Susannah Tolliver on a census in Indiana. The information is incomplete, they record. William's death records are also incomplete.

Jane Reeves remained in the employ of David Edwards Jr. after the trial. For approximately seven years, she tended to David and Elizabeth's children as well as Elizabeth the invalid. Jane grew impatient during those seven years. She had believed Elizabeth more ill than was the case, and on death's door, which was not the case. David did not believe his slaves were meant to care for them but simply there to work the farm. Therefore the work of cooking, cleaning and childcare was left to Jane.

During the birth of Elizabeth's and David's eleventh child, Elizabeth had a stroke leaving blindness in one eye and weakness in her right hand and right leg. Apparently, Jane was not aware of the incompleteness of her disability and believed her life was short-lived.

Thus, as Jane lost patience in getting what she had set her sights on, she decided to bring tea to Elizabeth on a regular basis. Elizabeth also preferred sugar in her tea.

Jane began taking the children to church every Sunday. David believed her to be a good, strong, God-fearing woman. Elizabeth began to feel the effects of the tea in completion after six weeks. Jane was fearful of using the same strength used on Susannah Tolliver as it would be detectable.

The children had become fond of Jane after seven years. David needed someone to care for the children. With their mother and his wife gone, he grew lonely as well. Jane was already living under their roof. She had moved in there, after her eight children had reached maturity to care for themselves. David's and Elizabeth's youngest daughter was but six years old when Jane moved into their home.

Jane was cooking his meals, cleaning his house and caring for his children. David believed a marriage contract was the most appropriate action under the circumstances.

David said to Jane one day, "Neither you nor I have likely prospects for remarriage. You need a home and I need a wife." It wasn't exactly what Jane had planned.

David was forty-four years of age and Jane was forty-one when they married. Together they had two children, Phoebe and Solomon.

Phoebe grew up to marry Dr. A.B. Cox who was a physician as well as a Methodist minister. After the death of her mother, Phoebe and her husband moved to Indiana and then eventually to Nebraska.

Dr. Cox later wrote a historical as well as a genealogical book called *Footprints on the Sands of Time* about northwestern North Carolina and southwestern Virginia.

There seems to be a battle over who actually wrote the famous spiritual poem, called "Footprints in the Sand." It was either Mary Stevenson, Carolyn Joyce Carty or Margaret Fishback-Powers. Regardless of who actually created the words, once again, we have a battle.

The poem is beautiful. It speaks to the truth that God is ever present in our lives. It is such a shame that there, too is a war over beauty and God.

One night I dreamed I was walking along the beach with the Lord.
Many scenes of my life flashed across the sky.
In each scene, I noticed footprints in the sand.
Sometimes, there were two sets of footprints,
Other times there were one set of footprints.

This bothered me because I noticed the low periods of my life,
When I was suffering anguish, sorrow or defeat,
I could only see one set of footprints.

So, I said to the Lord, "You promised me Lord, that if I followed you,
You would walk with me always.
But I have noticed that during the most trying periods of my life,
There have only been one set of footprints in the sand.
Why, when I needed you most, have you not been there for me?"
The Lord replied, "The times when you have
seen only one set of footprints,
Is when I carried you."

Footprints on the Sands of Time brings in a reference to time. It reminds us that the past does not just include one person's life but the many lives that passed before us. Perhaps each time we have struggled during any life it was God who intervened in a way to teach us the lesson we needed to learn. Susannah never made it to the beach to see her imprints in the sand, however, that does not mean she had no imprint on the sands of time.

We all have struggles. Life is not about those struggles, for life is not where we were but rather where we are heading. The footprints face forward not backward.

For if, indeed, in our times of struggle, God has carried us, it is because God believes in our potential. And, like any loving parent, God does not want us to fail.

Is this not the true definition of *ahav* and *ahava*?

So, when there are footprints in the sand, this is also a metaphor. Each imprint or step could be one moment, or one life in the journey of the soul.

Imagine how many steps there have been between the original David from the Mount of Olives to reach David Edwards Jr. of

North Carolina? And, how many steps or lives did it take between Ariela and Susannah Tolliver?

Lessons Learned in this lifetime...

- Conceit, jealousy and selfishness can poison love.

- Marriage is never a contract of convenience but rather a contract of love.

- Position does not change the truth. Murder is murder regardless of a technicality.

- Women and men are not to be owned or possessed. We give ourselves because we want to and not because we are expected to obey.

- Perhaps William Tolliver living a lie in that life staying under the radar, led to him living a lie in another life in another form. A lie is a lie regardless of how you disguise it.

- An early death does not allow for completion of one's path, causing reseeding.

Chapter 17
How Does Good & Evil Relate to Karma & God?

We just discussed in the last chapter the formation of the concepts of Good and Evil. These are very human concepts. They are concepts based on human, religious or philosophical opinions. Their basis is on value which is based on perspective. The problem lies in that these are all human perspectives. The issue remains that the only perspective that matters is God's.

Who is God, by the way? Let's examine what the Bible says. One of the first stories to consider in the Bible is the Prodigal Son. This is the story of the father who chooses to welcome home his son despite the son's mistakes. This resembles our story with God. We are given chance after chance to go home although we have made negative choices.

God discusses himself in Exodus. It reads as follows: *I am who I am* and, *this is my name, Yahweh.* This name translates to Lord in English. If we look as to how God describes himself, he literally says, *I exist and this is my name.*

Genesis claims *God as the creator.* In Genesis 1:3, *And God said, let there be light and there was light and God saw the light and it was good.* We have a story of a God so powerful that his mere voice created all that exists.

Revelations describes God as the *alpha and omega, the first and the last, the beginning and the end.* Revelations states that we have a God that always was and will always be.

1 John 4:8 states, *Anyone who does not love does not know God, because God is love.* Here, God is described as love.

Deuteronomy 7:9, *Know therefore that the lord your God is God, the faithful God who keeps covenant and steadfast love with those who love him and keep his commandments.* God appears to be fair and consistent in this scripture.

Isaiah 41:10, *Fear not for I am with you; be not dismayed, for I am your God; I will strengthen you, I will help you, I will uphold you with my righteous right hand.* God has told us many times in the Bible such as here, not to be scared, because he will always help us.

Deuteronomy 4:31, *For the Lord your God is a merciful God. He will not leave you or destroy you or forget the covenant with your fathers that he swore to them.* God is forgiving. He will not forsake you.

Exodus 34:6-7, *The Lord passed before him and proclaimed, the Lord, the Lord, a God merciful and gracious, slow to anger, and abounding in steadfast love and faithfulness. Forgiving iniquity and transgression and sin, but who will by no means clear the guilty visiting the iniquity of the fathers on the children and the children's children to the third and fourth generation.* This sounds like karma and reincarnation. We're given chance after chance to create positive karma and if we produce negative karma, it shows in our descendants even if those descendants are us. It will show in generations to come. We created it.

Joshua 1:9, *Have I not commanded you? Be strong and courageous, do not be frightened, and do not be dismayed, for the Lord your God is with you wherever you go.* No matter how bad our lives seem, God never abandons or forgets us.

Psalm 145:9, *The Lord is good to all and his mercy is over all that he has made.* God is fair to all not just a select few. God is following a fair plan for each of us. If you die at birth vs. dying at ninety, you have another chance for positive karma.

Isaiah 55:8-9, *For my thoughts are not your thoughts, neither are your ways, my ways, declares the Lord. For as the heavens are higher than the Earth, so are my ways higher than your ways and my thoughts higher than your thoughts.* Karma may be a bit difficult to comprehend. It's not really about bad and good but rather progress to full potential.

Isaiah 57:15, *For thus says the one who is high and lifted up, who inhabits eternity, whose name is holy: I dwell in the high and holy place and also with him who is of a contrite and lowly spirit, to revive the spirit of the lowly and revive the heart of the contrite.* God is available to everyone.

Ephesians 4:6, *One God and Father of all, who is overall and through all and in all.* We are all part of God and his creation.

Romans 12:19, *Dearly beloved, avenge not yourself but rather give place unto wrath: for it is written, vengeance is mine, I will repay, saith the Lord.*

Vengeance is a word filled with emotion. Most of us relate it to anger or revenge. Actually, the word vengeance would best be described as retribution. Thus, the above quote would be that *retribution is mine, saith the Lord.* In no way is God's retribution filled with anger or revenge.

Again, like any parent, it is simply about learning the lessons.

If you search for the meaning of the antonym for vengeance, you will ironically find it to mean the giving of forgiveness and grace.

Most of good and evil has been defined by man. Even the above passages were somewhat defined by man as they observed God.

At the end of creation, God looked at all he had made and said, *it is very good*. By this statement, we must believe that God created all, as he intended. Thus, God's plan must include free choice by man/woman that moves us either farther away from God or closer to God. Man has interpreted that which puts us farther from God as evil. However, God has said that everything he created was good also giving us free will. Our choices, the ones we deem poor or evil because they take us farther from God are necessary for growth. In fact, they must exist. They must exist because God allows it. It is part of God's creation. So, thus, just like the pull of karma will bring you back to people in another life, the literal pull of God's positive karma will sooner or later pull you back to God. It was always God's plan. One should think great comfort would be achieved, knowing that God is always watching and taking care of us. God's goal is the union with us in the end.

Chapter 18
The Quest

What do we know historically, thus far? We know that many religions believe in reincarnation. We know that reincarnation has been systematically removed from some religions.

We know that the New Testament was written years after Jesus's life and mostly by hearsay. We also know that the church set doctrine based on how it strengthened the church rather than by strengthening of God.

The church became the gatekeeper of God and spokesperson for God. The church also became the way to salvation, literally removing our responsibility completely and laying it on the plate of Jesus.

Thomas Merton, mentioned before, a Catholic-Buddhist monk of this century, believed that we had our own personal responsibility to reach our potential, without depending on others to achieve it for us.

He wrote many books about his meditation practices, understanding and religious thoughts. He proposed that there were two parts to salvation; God's part, grace and man's/woman's part which is reaching our potential.

We know the definition of good and evil based on man's perspective and not God's perspective. Evil is something that hurts us but evil is also something that focuses on "I" and is not based on "others." Good is based on "others" and not on "ourselves." Evil is based on making negative choices which bring us further from God or the light. And, good is based on positive choices and that which brings us closer to God and further from the darkness.

The evidence for reincarnation may seem circumstantial but not any more so than mainstream religion. Is it less believable than thinking we are responsible for our own actions or is it more believable to think that a man was born, died and took responsibility for all of our actions making us off the hook for everything? And, if there are thousands of people experiencing past lives while meditating or through regression, how can we look the other way and ignore it and pretend it isn't so, just because we weren't raised to believe it?

NDEs (near-death experiences) and past-life regression have so much in common, how can we discard it?

From the history of mankind, if a place like HELL exists, it must be brimming at the seams with people and Heaven must be a lonely place. God must not think fairly because the church preaches that only by being reborn in Jesus's name, can you be saved. And it seems a little arbitrary that if you were born before Jesus's time, you were grandfathered in.

Even in the Bible itself, in the Old Testament, God continues to remind the Jews that, "I am present and I realize you have screwed up but I'll give you another chance." So, the story for four thousand years has been, if you screwed up, I'll give you another chance and after Jesus, God supposedly quit giving us chances. The church says that only through the church with Jesus's help can you be saved and this is your last chance. It appears that God is saying, "I created you so miserably, I think, I'll kill myself, for it is I who has failed you." Maybe, in Genesis, instead of saying, "And it was good," God should have said, "It wasn't all so good."

Maybe God really did not stop talking to us. Maybe God did not give up on us. And maybe God still loves us. For this is a relationship. It is both ways. God would not turn his proverbial back on us even though that could be God's choice. Just as God wants us to make choices to not turn our backs on God, if we have, we have the choice to turn back around again.

For if God is love, God would not turn his back on us. Yet, we are given choice; at least by the church's stance we are. Because whatever choices you made before Jesus's time was forgiven and you will be returned to your rotten, six-thousand-year-old corpse. Maybe in some way the Gnostics were correct. We are all nothing but the walking dead with a need to be reborn into the light. We've heard so many humans say, "So, help me God." Maybe God finally has.

If God is love, it should be easy to see that turning away from conceit, selfishness, jealousy and unforgiveness is the same as turning toward God.

So, maybe the Zen Buddhists have something here. Removing ourselves from our thinking, or in other words, detachment from the "I" removes conceit, selfishness, jealousy and unforgiveness. If we do not dwell on our suffering, pain and negative circumstances then our perceptions of evil also change. We'll be able to see the positive results that stem from negative situations. We will see the growth in ourselves and others.

There have been six past-life stories in this book so far. They began with an account of a story filled with hope, ahav and ahava, meaning to give and to truly love. They pass through conflicts that end with a story filled with nothing less than deceit and lies. Thus, we enter our current lives again, our twenty-ninth time together, filled with conflict. Once again, this life is with ahav and ahava, yet we ask ourselves if we are able to reach our potential, rid ourselves of choices based on conceit, selfishness, jealousy and unforgiveness and reach the potential created in us by God.

If nature must evolve and nature was created by God and we were created by God, then shouldn't we be expected to evolve as well? And, we needed something, as in a soul or a seed, to record our evolution because evolution does not occur in just one lifetime.

So, as not to disappoint, here is one additional past-life story of our lives together, from Ariela and David to Carin and Darin, filled with hope and love.

■　■　■　■　■　■　■　■

The Quest ...
We write this story, ironically, on May 1st which is May Day or Beltane

Nearly seven hundred years had passed since Esther traveled to northern France. Esther's parents and her grandfather had been great healers.

Esther continued to pass down her gift and knowledge of healing to her daughters and they passed the healing gift and knowledge onto their daughters. The gift of love and healing passed through generation and generation.

Respect grew with this knowledge in a truly feminine inheritance. The female was creative and closer to nature. God was then seen as creative, feminine and one with nature.

We hesitate to call this group Wiccan. The Wiccan religion is one of the oldest religions and misunderstood. It is now believed to be a religion full of spells, demons, witches and the such when, in fact, it is a religion of respect for nature and creation. Like so many other religions of this world, it has been reinterpreted by society as what it was never intended to be. In this Celtic region of northern France, the Wiccans were nothing more than female priests and healers.

This healing cult of Wiccans believed their healing ability was passed down their soul lines. They also believed the greatest healers to be reincarnations of former healers. The rebirth in spring was representative of their rebirth, just as the flower, such as the rose, rebloomed. They, too, would rebloom in the future.

During this time, the Druids also existed in northern France. The Druids were a male, priestly order of the Celts.

The Celtic people were nothing more than a group of nomads or vagabonds, settling around Europe from 600 BC to the present day. They existed independent and prior to Christianity.

Their religion was based on a love of nature, the manifestations of God through nature and their differing beliefs of one God or many. The true difference was whether the main God directed the lesser Gods of nature or whether those Gods acted independently.

The Druids were the learned sect within the Celtic people. They were the leaders politically, religiously, academically and culturally. And, of course, they were all male.

The Druids expressed a belief in the spirit of man/woman and the belief that the spirit did not die. They believed the soul moved onto another life. In fact, the Celtic knot is a symbol for two lovers who lived together in one life, died and came back together as two adjacent trees. The two trees intertwined in such a way there could be no differentiation in where the trees began and ended, together blended as one. They also believed their lineage or ancestry to be important because it was believed our soul or spirit could be reincarnated through our lineage; the same soul to be reborn into the same family over and over again. The Druids saw this cycle of rebirth, acknowledged in nature all around them.

However, the Druids saw the lesser Gods of being both female and male. Thus, those believing in a greater God, believed that God had both characteristics as female and male.

The two groups, the Wiccans and the Druids, existed without conflict. Believing themselves all to be Celtic.

The Wiccans respected the Druids for their knowledge and likewise the Druids the Wiccans for their knowledge of healing.

Thirty-four generations after Esther, Carin was born to a Druid father and a Wiccan mother. Darin was born to a Druid father and a Celtic woman. (A woman could not be a Druid, therefore, his mother was referred to as Celtic only).

Darin's father ran a school for Druid teachings, and much to the community's disdain, admitted females. Carin was enrolled by her mother and father. Both children began their training at around the age of seven.

One of the favored games at the Druid school was played using a twelve-sided dice, each side of the dice was one inch in length, twelve sides of the dice were considered a foot. Holes were drilled in the dice. When the dice was held to the sky, the holes would line up to the constellations, representing twelve faces of God in the zodiac. This twelve-sided dice could be used to measure during planting season based on how many inches the rows should be planted apart. When the dice aligned correctly with the constellations, it meant the right time to plant the crops. It also explained, since the constellations were changing based on the time of the year, why they decided on twelve months to a year. It was also believed that a person's characteristics could be based on which face of God they were born under. They could not build a twelve-faced dice without a five-sided face in each. Thus, as the two cultures merged as one, the five-sided pentagon became associated with the Wiccan women (not witches as later believed). Because, if you drew the picture of a man or woman, they both had two arms, two legs and a head, equaling five. All five sides were equal. Thus, men and women should be equal. The pentagon with five equal sides became synonymous with the belief that Wiccan women were equal to Druid men (not the sign of witches).

The Celtics, as nomads, spread the dodecahedron dice throughout Europe where it was discovered eventually by the Romans during their conquests. Apparently, the Celtics are the originators of the dodecahedron with God.

A molding together of the Druid and Wiccan beliefs began. A multifaceted, single God, represented by nature and the heavens, based on the cycles of life or nature, with both equally feminine and masculine attributes, was created.

The last issue to be resolved between the two cultures was sacrifice of any kind. The creative nature of the Wiccans could not comprehend or understand the destruction of God's creation under any circumstances. The Druids had long sacrificed for blessings of the harvest, the God's favor in storms, strength to overcome their enemies and anything else requiring help from the Gods.

The Druid belief of sacrifice was based on a strange theory that because some of the faces of God were storms, that God was somehow vengeful or required something from us.

A statement by Carin, a young, seven-year-old Wiccan girl, stuck with Darin. She said, "If God provides creation for us out of love, is it not love that God expects from us?"

This began the friendship of the two young children. Over the next six years, their education continued in the Druid school.

One day at school, Darin asked the question, "Why does God allow storms if he is not vengeful?" And Carin, being a practical thinker, responded, "Do not the storms bring rain? Does the rain not allow the flowers and crops to bloom? Does your teaching not tell you that two lovers will return and bind into one tree? This does not seem like a vengeful God."

Darin's father, seeing the wisdom of the Wiccan child, thought my son must be exposed to the Wiccan teachings. He also believed if God was also the realm of women, the realm of healing must also be of men. He expressed his belief's to Carin's mother.

Carin's mother contacted her sister, also the aunt of Carin. She requested that both Carin and Darin be enrolled in her herbal school of healers. They were twelve years of age.

Even though Darin and Carin were great friends, at first Carin was somewhat suspect of the few young boys attending the school at that time. Carin wondered if boys could really be caretakers. However, Darin excelled at identifying flowers, herbs and roots.

Carin's feelings for Darin started to change, when he rescued an injured, nestling Puffin, fallen to the ground. He fed, watered and cared for the nestling. He spent hours trying to teach the Puffin to dive and swim. One day, the Puffin finally flew away. She saw both a smile and a tear as Darin watched the results of his efforts of love. She thought to herself, "Certainly, he is in touch with his feminine side and he, too, can nurture."

As they approached the end of their training, Darin also noticed how Carin was blossoming in another way, other than healing. Spring was approaching and graduation would be celebrated on the festival of Beltane. Darin and Carin had been schooling as herbalists for six years.

A large pole with two woven ropes was erected in the middle of the grounds. There were flowers attached to the woven ropes and the pole in celebration of May Day. All of the graduates from the herbal school alternated in dancing around the pole. Darin and Carin were each attached to one of the ropes on the pole at the same time. As they went round and around the pole, the rope became shorter and tightened. It soon brought both of their wrists together.

One of their teachers, Carin's aunt, cut a portion of the now-twisted ropes from each of their ropes. She tied their ropes together in a Celtic Knot.

Celtic knots are complete loops having no start or finish and could be said to be representative of eternity in loyalty, faith, friendship and love. One thread is normally used in each design to symbolize the interconnectedness of life and eternity.

Thus, became the blending of two lives, two souls, two religious thoughts and two, but one love.

Lessons learned in this lifetime...

- The real lesson is that perhaps there is some truth in all religions. Our quest is to somehow find a way of blending our thoughts and beliefs together as one. If we look carefully, that common rope or thread is love.

Although our journey began years ago, our sense of urgency in quest, began in 2014.

We both were initially raised in Catholicism. However, it did not answer our questions and it became readily apparent we had a need for more answers than, "Just believe and have faith." We began reading historical and religious books including the Bible and the Quran. We explored other religions.

We began to use meditation for stress relief later in our adult years and discovered more than just relaxation and clearing our minds. We experienced memories and these memories were unique in that they did not occur in this lifetime. This led us to more knowledge about meditation and more about past lives and reincarnation. We documented thirty-four lives for Carla and forty-two lives for Dave. Twenty-nine of these lives were together.

We trained in past-life regression with Dr. and Mrs. Brian Weiss, as well as other courses on hypnosis.

We continued to ask questions, meditate, investigate and educate ourselves about the subject of reincarnation and past lives.

We found a common thread throughout those lives. Conceit, selfishness, jealousy and unforgiveness cannot be found in pure love.

We found an intertwining of past lives with people currently around us. There was no way, as complicated and intricate as these lives were, that they could occur only by chance. It was obvious to us that God is not dead, quiet or absent and is still available and active in all of our lives.

About the Authors

Dave and Carla, the authors, want to share their spiritual journey by sharing their story, with the world.

They teach Meta Meditation and *The Five Simple Rules for Living* which are to live without **conceit, jealousy, selfishness** and with **forgiveness** and **love**.

Through training with Dr. and Mrs. Brian Weiss they learned the art of regression therapy at the Omega Institute and use meditation along, with hypnosis to help others grow and explore their own past lives

Their first book, *The Gift of Past Lives with Mother, Isabella, God & Elizabeth* takes the reader through twenty-one of their past lives together. The Five Simple Rules are outlined in detail. These rules help the reader evaluate their past and current lives thus releasing them from the chains that bind them.

Dave and Carla are soon to release their third book. Watch for it on one of our sites.

Visit: **thegiftofpastlives.com**… to find out more and read excerpts from their first book.

Follow the authors on **Facebook** at *Mother, Isabella, God & Elizabeth* or on our discussion group at *Past Lives with Mother, Isabella, God & Elizabeth.*

Made in the USA
Columbia, SC
28 September 2020